Models For Critical Thinking

*A Fundamental Guide to Effective Decision Making,
Deep Analysis, Intelligent Reasoning, and
Independent Thinking*

Written by Albert Rutherford

Copyright © 2018 Albert Rutherford. All rights reserved.

All rights reserved. No part of this publication may be reproduced, distributed, or transmitted in any form or by any means, including photocopying, recording, or other electronic or mechanical methods, without the prior written permission of the publisher, except in the case of brief quotations embodied in critical reviews and certain other noncommercial uses permitted by copyright law. For permission requests, contact the author.

Limit of Liability/ Disclaimer of Warranty: The author makes no representations or warranties with respect to the accuracy or completeness of the contents of this work and specifically disclaims all warranties, including without limitation warranties of fitness for a particular purpose. No warranty may be created or extended by sales or promotional materials. The advice contained herein may not be suitable for everyone. This work is sold with the understanding that the author is not engaged in rendering medical, legal or other professional advice or services. If professional assistance is required, the services of a competent professional person should be sought. The author shall not be liable for damages arising therefrom.

The fact that an individual, organization of website is referred to in this work as a citation and/or potential source of further information does not mean that the author endorses the information the individual, organization to website may provide or recommendations they/it may make. Further, readers should be aware that Internet websites listed in this work might have changed or disappeared between when this work was written and when it is read.

First Printing, 2018.
ISBN: 9781728892245

Printed in the United States of America

Published by Kindle Direct Publishing

Email: albertrutherfordbooks@gmail.com

Website: www.albertrutherford.com

If you wish to receive notifications from me twice a month about:

- new book releases,

- new cognitive discoveries I made,

- book recommendations on how to develop your thinking toolkit further,

- ideas I'm pondering on,

visit www.albertrutherford.com and fill in the subscribe box.

Thank you! Talk to You soon.

Table of Contents

Chapter 1: What Is Critical Thinking?.................13
   Qualities And Benefits Of Critical Thinkers 17
   Why Use Critical Thinking? 22
   Thinking Hiccups 26
   What Creates Your Beliefs?.. 30

Chapter 2: What Isn't Critical Thinking?...........35
   Distinguishing Between Non-Critical, Weakly Critical, And Strongly Critical Thinking.............. 36
   Uncritical-Illogical Thinking 39
   Statistics Vs. Stereotypes 0-1 45
   In Defense Of Uncritical Thinking 53
   Cognitive Biases.. 55

Chapter 3: How Are Our Thoughts Influenced? 65
   Indoctrination 68
   Dark Lessons From Nazism 74
   Spot The Persuasion Techniques Used On You 83

Chapter 4: Learning Models For Critical Thinking 93
- Bloom's Taxonomy 93
- The SOLO Taxonomy 103
- Bloom's Taxonomy Versus SOLO Taxonomy .. 104
- Paul-Elder Critical Thinking Framework.......... 106
- Occam's Razor 120

Chapter 5: Critical Thinking As Dr. Kahneman Knows 125
- Intuition And Expertise 127
- Jumping To Conclusions 131

Chapter 6: Staying Clear Of Thinking Errors .. 141
- Data – Information- Knowledge – Understanding - Wisdom 141
- How To Detect Biases When We Transform Data Into Information? 148
- De-Biasing 151

Chapter 7: Critical Reading And Writing 159
- Critical Reading 159
- Critical Writing 173

Chapter 8: Empower Your Logic Toolkit 185

Unnecessary And Insufficient 194
What Are Hidden Assumptions? 197
The Laws Of Thought By Aristotle 199
What Makes An Argument Convincing? 203
Recognizing Fallacies 207
Logic Exercises 211

Chapter 9: Reasoning By Analogy 219
Introducing Reasoning By Analogy 219
The Power Of Words 221
Uncovering False Analogies 225
Analogy In Practice 227
Practice Your Analogy Skills 231

Chapter 10: Critical Thinking Hall Of Fame 235
Critical Thinking Lessons From The Greatest Thinkers Of The World: 235
Arguments That Changed Our World 240

Closing 249

Reference 253

Endnotes 269

Chapter 1: What is Critical Thinking?

"The philosopher Richard Paul has described three kinds of people: vulgar believers, who use slogans and platitudes to bully those holding different points of view into agreeing with them; sophisticated believers, who are skilled at using intellectual arguments, but only to defend what they already believe; and critical believers, who reason their way to conclusions and are ready to listen to others."

– Carole Wade and Carol Tavris

According to the dictionary, critical thinking is the process of actively and skillfully conceptualizing, applying, analyzing, synthesizing, and evaluating information to reach an answer or conclusion.[i] In other words, critical thinking is an attempt to dig deeper and get beyond a superficial understanding of things by asking good questions, examining words, being sensitive to the context words are written in, understanding the feelings and emotions behind them, and being generally open minded. It is a quest to understand the reason behind people's thoughts and a refusal to accept things at face value without making sure they are supported by facts and evidence, even if it takes questioning an authority figure to achieve this.

Critical thinkers want to examine other possible explanations and options instead of only being satisfied with the first one they come across. They not only question the conclusions people make, but also the assumptions at the root of these conclusions. Logic is valued over gut feelings and intuition. Critical thinkers want to see the proofs that lead to the conclusion before they are willing to believe it.

Just because someone thinks something does not automatically make it true.

Thinking and knowing are not the same things. A healthy dose of skepticism can be beneficial when it comes to uncovering reason. Critical thinkers are willing to question what they hear on the news, from authority figures, as well as people in their lives whom they respect. They even question their own words and thoughts in their search for concrete knowledge and unbiased answers.

If critical thinking was only about drawing logical conclusions, we could input an algorithm into a computer and all of our problems would be solved, but thinking critically is so much more than that. Critical thinkers are keenly aware of the ways words are used and the role feelings and emotions play in guiding people to reach certain conclusions.

As humans, we all come with our own baggage, filled with biases and preconceived notions. As critical thinkers, we understand this and recognize how our biases can get in the way of finding the best answers. With the help of critical thinking, we can make a conscious effort to not only uncover these biases in others that may lead them to draw certain conclusions, but also to check our own biases at the door when we examine information and arguments.

Using critical thinking, we can become open-minded enough to accept new evidence even when it goes against something we currently believe. We recognize that beliefs are not absolute, but rather works in progress that can, and should, evolve and change over time.

Some people are willing to accept the first argument that is presented to them or give up when it seems there is only one explanation or option. Not critical thinkers. They will keep digging until they find a solid idea or option based on evidence.

Qualities and benefits of critical thinkers

Critical thinking requires additional cognitive effort on our part instead of blindly following the beliefs of others or the first thoughts that come to our minds. What benefits do we get in return for our cognitive efforts?

- We become more open-minded and tolerant of people with viewpoints that are different from our own. We welcome the ideas of others and view them as an opportunity to learn something new. Life can be boring if there are no challenges to our thinking and we are content to just maintain the status quo. Critical thinking encourages us to undergo these challenges and relish a good debate.
- We will see events through a more analytical lens. We won't be willing to accept things at face value. Our interest will be in finding

good arguments supported by strong evidence and reason.

- We will become confident enough to challenge even conventional views if significant evidence suggests that they may be outdated and no longer useful, or not based on relevant evidence.
- We become curious people who have an insatiable desire to find better answers. We'll become willing to follow facts wherever they may lead us, even if it means we need to adapt or abandon our beliefs when we are presented with new quality information.
- We'll be able to read between the lines and dig deeper to find the hidden or implied meaning behind the words. Critical thinking requires a lifelong dedication to learn.
- We'll be able to examine written text with a sharp eye, looking for the biases of the author, or the publishing company. We'll also become more proficient in critical writing, the

usage of our words will become more accurate, focused, and descriptive of the point we want to make.

We have the ability to think and act rationally – Aristotle called us 'rational animals' - but we don't always take advantage of this gift. Too often we are willing to cling to our beliefs, even when they aren't based on anything else but our emotions, gut feelings, or worse - the emotions and gut feelings of others. Logic, reasoning, and evidence don't play any role in these beliefs. Many of our beliefs are rooted in faulty information that could easily be disproved if we were willing to question it. Once the faulty information is found to be false, the belief would naturally change.

We are adept at coming up with explanations why we hold the beliefs or make the choices we do. Often we come up with those reasons to convince ourselves as much as others. For example, when we decide to upgrade to the latest smartphone, we may say we are doing it for the improved camera or faster processing speed that allows us to get more done for our job when we are on the go. When in reality, we want to upgrade to keep up with everyone else and we may even see having the latest technology at our fingertips as a status symbol. You and I both know that social media and emails don't require the type of technology available on the latest smartphones and for shooting good photos, a traditional camera is still better.

We have a natural tendency to allow our irrational sides to take control. Unless we make a conscious decision to overcome it, we'll be hijacked by the illogical side of our brain and be exposed to the mercy of the odds when we choose to do (or not do) something based on irrational reasoning. We will examine this in depth later in the book.

Critical thinkers can understand how ideas are connected and evaluate whether information and arguments are relevant and important to addressing the issues at hand. They can build arguments to defend their own beliefs as well as recognize and examine the arguments of others. They can spot gaps in information and errors in the reasoning that lead to conclusions, approaching things calmly and objectively knowing that they are prepared to take things one step at a time until they find the knowledge they seek.

The American Psychology Association Expert Consensus on Critical Thinking has identified the following characteristics as being present in strong critical thinkers:[ii]

- curiosity toward a variety of issues,
- desire to be well-informed and a lifelong learner,
- awareness of situations when critical thinking may be beneficial,
- confidence in their own reasoning skills,
- receptive to learning from people with viewpoints that differ from their own,

- openness to a variety of beliefs and opinions,
- objective and fair when analyzing arguments and reasoning,
- recognition of their own biases and prejudices that may cloud their judgment,
- reservation of judgment until they have examined all of the facts,
- willingness to reevaluate their beliefs and adjust or abandon them if they are presented with evidence that justifies it.

Why Use Critical Thinking?

Too often people blindly accept the beliefs of others and they can't explain why they believe what they do or what evidence supports those beliefs. People become completely attached to these beliefs and they don't like to have them challenged. Critical thinkers do the opposite.

Some people are resistant to adjust or abandon incorrect or outdated beliefs even when they are presented with evidence that disproves them. Their approach to improving their understanding of an issue is to begin by arguing then attempting to come up with reasons that support their point of view. Critical thinkers do the steps in reverse. First they look for logical reasons and evidence and they analyze the collected data, finally they engage in arguments using the conclusions they've made after the analysis.

Types of thinkers

Charles Sanders Peirce, a 19th century American philosopher and logician, identified three kinds of thinkers:

1. Sticklers: These are people who cling tightly to their beliefs regardless of any new evidence that may come along to refute them. They are only interested in information or opinions that can serve to support their own views and easily dismiss or ignore any ideas that stand in opposition to them.

2. Followers: These are thinkers who happily base their beliefs on what they think authority figures support. If there is no authority figure present, they will go along with whatever they think the majority of people agree with. They do not question the wisdom of experts or the consensus of many and often just accept those opinions blindly as being truth. Followers can be helpful in creating a feeling of unity and connection, but they can also be easily persuaded to go with the flow in negative circumstances such as following a dangerous leader or joining in and bullying someone. Followers are unlikely to generate their own original ideas and opinions because there seems to be too much of a risk for error in their mind.

3. System Builders: These thinkers are willing to accept new information as long as they can make it fit within the general understanding

and framework that they already have. If they would have to totally reject the way they have viewed the world and the logical structure they have created for themselves that supports their understanding, they would much rather ignore the new information than completely abandon their worldview.[iii]

Have you ever tried to follow the advice of a book only to discover half way through that the author was wrong, had strong biases which he seemingly was unaware of, so you decided it would be best to stop reading and choose another book instead? If so, you just might be a critical thinker. Peirce believed that we should look at the world as though it was entirely possible that everything we thought we knew and believed might be wrong and be willing to start over from scratch if we needed to.

Another American philosopher, William James, felt the same when he pointed out that people often believed they were thinking critically when what they were really doing was just moving their prejudices around. They might have been basing their views on emotions without evidence to support them. He recognized that critical thinkers seek to first become more aware of their own biases so that they can consciously work to overcome them and be more objective and open-minded.[iv]

Critical thinking skills don't come naturally. They require effort and must be modeled and taught. We can't just assume that people automatically know how to think critically.

Thinking hiccups

The Nobel Prize Winner and American professor, Daniel Kahneman, believes that people are "irrational animals" who are susceptible to making mistakes and incorrect judgments. He thinks people are innately illogical and prone to thinking errors when they evaluate situations in largely predictable patterns.

Kahneman believes the human brain is hardwired to think in irrational ways because throughout history our very survival depended on it, so it became our instinct and part of our nature.[v] Think about how much time our ancestors had to evaluate their best escape options when a hungry predator was chasing them. They didn't analyze anything, they just ran as fast as they could and climbed the first tree they found. They didn't have time to stop, look around, and find the tallest tree or the one with the most branches that made climbing easy. If they were mentally present enough, they assessed if the predator could climb the tree or not, and chose other escape options.

Kahneman identifies human thinking as being either logical or instinctual. He states it is during times of instinctual thinking when we make most of our mistakes in judgment. Our brains don't like it when we are faced with gaps in information and it is eager to close those gaps. We are content to jump at the first choice or solution that comes along without taking the time to fully assess the consequences that may come along with it.

We have access to more information than at any other point in human history, but it can be too much for our brains to take in and properly sort through. Not to mention that being exposed to information all day long does no good to our judgment when we cannot tell who is reporting fact and who is reporting fiction. Our brains search for patterns and connections to the beliefs we already have and information we already know. There are times when this can prove helpful, but there are also times when this instinctual type of thinking can lead us astray by encouraging us to jump to conclusions without taking the time to gather all of the facts available to us.

The brain consumes more energy than any other human organ – nearly twenty percent of our total energy haul even though the brain generally accounts for only two percent of our total body mass.[vi] We naturally try to conserve energy when we can, so you can imagine why the brain would instinctively try to avoid going into deep thought as much as possible. This is why we rely so much on old familiar patterns when it comes to making judgments and decisions. We try to reach conclusions quickly. When we solve problems too fast, we often end up coming to the wrong conclusion or settling for the easy fix instead of the best outcome. These hasty solutions can even bring with them unintended negative consequences that we didn't account for.

Let's try a math problem to help illustrate this theory. Together a bat and ball cost $1.10. The bat costs $1.00 more than the ball. How much does the ball cost? Take a minute to consider your answer.

If you are like most people, you probably think the ball costs 10 cents. If that were true, the bat would cost $1.10 because the problem stated that the bat cost $1.00 more than the ball. This would mean that the total cost of the bat and ball would be $1.20. The correct answer is that the ball costs 5 cents and the bat costs $1.05, adding up to a total of $1.10.

The math is not terribly difficult so why do the majority of us get the answer wrong? In order to quickly solve the problem, the brain often tries to replace a harder problem with an easier one. The math problem stated that the bat cost $1.00 more than the ball, but in order to make things simple, the brain may have mistakenly substituted that information with the idea that the bat cost $1.00, which leads to a quick, but incorrect, judgment that the ball cost 10 cents. This is a prime example of how our instinct to find a quick and easy answer can lead us astray.

What creates your beliefs?

Deanna Kuhn conducted research about how much control people exercise over making their own decisions versus how much control they relinquish by just being a follower and going along with the opinions of others. Critical thinkers base their beliefs, choices, and judgments on evidence, but Kuhn found that most people are unable to cite evidence to back up their reasoning for holding their beliefs. Further, many people refuse to modify or abandon their beliefs, even when they are presented with new reliable information that disproves them.[vii]

There is a theory often used in the social sciences to explain how many people come to make choices or decisions called informational cascade. This theory explains that people often rely on the choices of others to guide their decision-making rather than gathering evidence to make an informed choice. This may be due to lack of time or the inability to find the facts on their own. Decisions are made on observations of the choices of others while ignoring their own personal information. In many cases, it's easier to go along with the ideas of the crowd.[viii]

There are times when following information that others share is perfectly rational. Like following the advice of financial experts and creating an emergency savings account. But often you could follow the wrong information and make irrational choices based on biased or incomplete information such as participating in a ridiculous and dangerous challenge on social media or following an unhealthy fad diet.

We have all heard the toothpaste commercials that claim their product is preferred or recommended by eight out of ten dentists. This is a powerful marketing tool that capitalizes on the informational cascade of how people often allow the choices of others or the advice of experts to guide their decision-making. It would be easy to assume that since dentists are experts in their field, their recommendation should carry a lot of weight when we decide which toothpaste to purchase.

However, the Advertising Standards Authority banned this slogan from being used by the Colgate toothpaste company in 2007 as it was determined to be a misleading claim and a breach of advertising rules. The company involved conducted a telephone survey of dentists, but they allowed the dentists to recommend more than one brand of toothpaste which resulted in another toothpaste company achieving the same high number of recommendations as Colgate. Just because we are told that nearly all experts agree, there may be much more to the story.[ix]

Blindly following the advice of experts or the consensus of a group abdicates our decision-making power to others and often prevents us from making an objective, rational, informed decision based on evidence for ourselves. Applying our critical thinking skills can go a long way toward avoiding misleading information like this.

Chapter 2: What Isn't Critical Thinking?

Now that we have a better understanding of what critical thinking is, in this chapter we will examine what it isn't.

Some people think that critical thinking has to be very formal and that its primary goal is to try to poke holes into the arguments and reasoning of others. Critical thinking is far more helpful in the real world, allowing us to make informed, quality decisions in a whole host of practical areas of our lives, like determining whether a choice we make is morally right or wrong, whether it would be more cost effective to fly or drive to our vacation destination, or what would be the most productive use of employee time on a new project at work.

While critical thinking does require a set of skills that need to be practiced and can be strengthened and improved over time, it goes far beyond just a list of study skills or strategies. Study skills are things that teachers tell students to do that can easily be memorized and applied. They give the basic knowledge tools that one can build on.

Critical thinking includes things like evaluating information to determine what is relevant to help solve the problem or recognizing bias that might interfere with the objectivity of a source of information.

Distinguishing between non-critical, weakly critical, and strongly critical thinking

We have access to so much information in our lives in both written and audiovisual formats. Not all sources are created equally and some are much more reliable than others. We can take one of three approaches when we evaluate the information that we encounter:

1. We can be **non-critical** and accept the information at face value exactly as it is presented to us. In this approach, we simply take in the information without trying to compare it to other sources, questioning it, or challenging its claims.

2. A second approach is to be **weakly critical**. This approach presumes that the overall reasoning and assumptions on which the information is based are largely sound, but it recognizes that there may be some incorrect conclusions drawn. In the example of taking a weakly critical look at a research study, we would dig a little deeper to examine if the sample size was an adequate representation, if sound universal research practices were followed, and if the conclusions drawn were logical. We would only accept the findings as

being reliable and valid if we are satisfied that the criteria we used to judge the study had sufficiently been met. In research reliability and validity are specific terms with specific meanings. Reliability is how consistent or accurate the measure used was. Validity is whether or not the measure used actually measured what it was intended to measure. Sometimes measures are not created well and the researcher might end up gathering data on the incorrect thing and the research becomes invalid.

3. We can approach information in a **strongly critical** manner, which is in essence, taking the information down to the "studs" in that we examine every aspect of it. We challenge and question its authority to make sure it is not just an isolated opinion and that its foundation is firmly evidence-based. We look for any biases the source has and examine the

assumptions that are made closely. We look for errors in reasoning and weak or incorrect conclusions. When we are strongly critical, we research to find other sources that either agree or refute the claims made.[x] The best measure of a research study is its ability to be repeated and the results recreated by other researchers.

Uncritical-illogical thinking

Sometimes we make mistakes in our logical reasoning and we draw incorrect conclusions. The mistakes we make are fairly predictable as we make them repeatedly because they are due in large part to how our brain is hardwired. We have to increase our awareness and work to overcome these common errors if we hope to strengthen our critical thinking skills.

Meet Linda

Amos Tversky and Daniel Kahneman are psychology professors known for their extensive work in studying human behavior, reasoning, and decision making. In 1983 they conducted a study on unintended bias in which they presented participants with the following problem:[xi]

"Linda is thirty-one years old, single, outspoken, and very bright. She majored in philosophy. As a student she was deeply concerned with issues of discrimination and social justice, and also participated in anti-nuclear demonstrations."

The professors gave the students a list of possible careers for Linda such as an elementary teacher, insurance salesperson, or a bookstore employee who takes yoga classes. They wanted to see if the participants would rely on preconceived stereotypes when it came to selecting the career they felt she was most likely to have.

Kahneman and Tversky then took a different approach and included this career on the list twice but presented it in different ways. They asked participants which of the following was more likely:

1. Linda is a bank teller.
2. Linda is a bank teller and is active in the feminist movement.

Tversky and Kahneman wrote the description of Linda in a way that made it seem likely that she would have been active in the feminist movement without including any specific information that would lead participants to believe she would be drawn to a career as a bank teller.

By connecting an outcome that participants considered likely (participation in the feminist movement) with an outcome that they would not have necessarily predicted on their own (career as a bank teller), it resulted in eighty-nine percent of the participants selecting the second outcome as being more likely than the first.

However, the participants' response demonstrated an error in reasoning because in order for the second outcome to be true, the first outcome automatically had to be true. Their thinking was illogical because the likelihood of two very specific things happening together in conjunction is *always* less than the likelihood of just one of those things happening by itself.

For example, imagine you were asked if it is more likely that you would be struck by lightning today or that you would be struck by lightning today while you were reading. Neither one is particularly likely, but the odds of you reading a book at the exact time of a thunderstorm makes the second outcome even a little less likely than the first. In order for the second outcome to be true, both the lightning strike and your presence with the book would have to occur simultaneously.

Tversky and Kahneman believe their findings prove the often illogical nature of human thinking. Our brain on energy saver mode causes us to fall back on relying on shortcuts to help us get to answers and solutions faster

There are others who think there is more to the case of Linda. They think that when the professors made the statement, "Linda is a bank teller and is active in the feminist movement" they caused people to interpret the other statement "Linda is a bank teller" as meaning Linda is a bank teller who is not active in the feminist movement.

They believe that the students viewed it difficult to predict Linda's career from the information given, so they saw the likelihood of her holding each career to be relatively close to one another statistically. But the information provided made them think that Linda would almost certainly be active in the feminist movement, so they were much more inclined to choose the prediction that she is a bank teller and a feminist. They see the participants' choices as something they can evaluate mathematically and as being based on some logic coupled with their intuition.

In the language of math, something either is or isn't happening, thus logically the possibility of Linda being something is fifty-fifty, (0.5). She either is or isn't something from the list of possibilities. We established that Linda being a bank teller is less likely, let's say, the chances are 1 in 100, (0.01). The probability of Linda being a feminist is extremely likely, 9 in 10, (0.9).

Thus the probability of Linda being simply a bank teller is 0.01x0.5= 0.005, 5 in 1000. Linda being a bank teller and a feminist, 0.01x0.9=0.009, or 9 in 1000. This is the logic that drives people's intuition in the language of math.

This reasoning goes against the "probability of a conjunction is never greater than the probability of its conjunctions" (P(A∩B)≤P(B)) but hey, this is also an explanation.

Statistics vs. stereotypes 0-1

Stereotypes...we all have them and use them mostly unconsciously. When it comes to stereotypes or statistics what do you think your gut thinking would be more likely to rely on to help you make decisions and solve problems? If you're like most people, the answer is most likely stereotypes. Why is that? A major reason is that many people simply don't understand statistics, so they rely on the easy and familiar shortcut. Critical thinkers are aware that they come with their own preconceived stereotypes and biases and work to keep them in check by identifying them and trying to overcome them through thoughtful and objective analysis of information.

The story of the eyewitness and the Bayesian Analysis

Eyewitness accounts aren't as reliable as we might think. Often two people can witness the exact same thing and come up with a very different description about it afterward. There are many factors that can contribute to this inaccuracy, such as the amount of stress the witness was under when they were in the situation. Or the fact that, even though we tend not to remember occurrences in accurate detail but rather the "gist" of what happened, over time we become more convinced of the accuracy of our memory as time passes. Or whether the witness was lead to make an identification through specifically worded questions or the interviewer's body language.

Bayesian analysis attempts to bring probability to statistics through math calculations. Consider Bayesian analysis of the following situation, which it calculates the likelihood of the accuracy of an eyewitness identification of a car involved in a hit and run accident.

In a city eighty-five percent of the cars are green and fifteen percent of them are blue. A witness identified the car involved in a hit and run accident as being blue. Most people would automatically assume that the car, which caused the accident, was blue due to the witness's statement.

The court tested the witness's ability to correctly identify colors and found that the witness correctly identified a car's color eighty percent of the time, but was incorrect twenty percent of the time. If we tell you that there is a twenty percent chance that the witness was incorrect when they identified the cab as being blue and eighty-five percent of the city's cars are green, you might change your level of confidence in the witness's description.[xii]

Bayesian theory states that given two events D (where D stands for data) and H (where H stands for hypothesis), the probability of D and H happening at the same time is the same as the probability of D occurring, given H, weighted by the probability that H occurs; or vice versa.[xiii] Written down, the formula looks like this:

$$P(H \cap D) = P(H|D)P(D) = P(D|H)P(H)$$

What is the data and the hypothesis? Using our intuitive thinking we may say that the proportion of the blue and green cars is the data and the witness' statement, that a blue car was responsible for the accident, is the hypothesis. If, however, we give some additional thought, we'll discover the following more accurate to find the answer to the part $P(H|D)$, where P stands for probability, the hypothesis being the accident was caused by a blue car, and the data being the witness said the car was blue.

Now all we need to do is replace the letters with numbers. We know that the probability of the car being blue is fifteen percent, P(H). (Why? Because the exercise started by stating that fifteen percent of the cars in town are blue) But what is P(D), the probability of the data? When would the witness state that the car was blue? In case of the car indeed being blue, or being actually green and the witness being wrong. Using the following calculation of the law of total probabilities:

P(D)=P(D|H)P(H)+P(D|¯H)P(¯H)=0.8•0.15+0.2•0.85 =0.29.

Since fifteen percent of the city's cars are blue, there is also a fifteen percent chance that this car was blue, there is an eighty percent chance that the color was correctly identified, so the combined probability is .15 * .8 = .12, or a twelve percent chance that the cab is blue.

There is an eighty-five percent chance that the car was green since eighty-five percent of the city's cars are green, and a twenty percent chance that the color was incorrectly identified, so the combined probability is .85 * .2 = .17, or a seventeen percent chance that the car was green.

Since the car had to be either blue or green, the witness could be expected to identify the car as being blue twenty-nine percent of the time whether she was right or wrong. This total probability of it being identified as blue was found by adding the two previously calculated percentages together .12 + .17 = .29. The chances she was right are .12 out of .29, or forty-one percent. Mathematically, there is a forty-one percent chance that the witness was correct and the car involved in the accident was blue.

Are they really smarter?
The SAT, Standardized Assessment Test, is the test taken by most students in the United States before

they enter college. It was designed to predict the future success of students in college, but some think it is a more accurate indicator of how wealthy students' families are.

In 2014, the average SAT score of college-bound students in the United States identified as being very poor (in families earning up to $20,000 per year) is 1326 points out of a possible 2400.[1] The average scores increase in conjunction with the income level of the students' families. Students from families earning $20,000-40,000 have an average score of just over 1400. The pattern continues to the highest level. Students from families earning $200,000 or more a year have average SAT scores of just over 1700 points.[xiv]

There are three ways to interpret this data:

---

[1] The SAT scoring format changed in 2016. The scoring for this test is now 1600 total points.

1. Wealthier students are smarter than poorer students. This interpretation assumes that the parents of the richer students are also smarter which enables them to earn greater incomes and they pass these genes along to their children.

2. Wealthier students receive a better education than poorer students. They are able to attend better schools and their parents can afford to hire tutors or enroll them in additional academic programs to help them if needed, so they are better prepared to take the test and perform better on the assessment.

3. The test is a measure of social class students are in as determined by their parents' incomes.

In defense of uncritical thinking

Psychologists identify mistakes people make in their reasoning as being part of two categories: motivational ("hot") illusions or cognitive ("cold") illusions.

"Hot" illusions occur when we let our feelings and emotions impact our reasoning. Most people predict that the beliefs and views they hold in the present will remain the same in the future. In reality, we are always growing, changing, and evolving, which means our viewpoint is likely to change over time as well.

"Cold" illusions are errors in thinking such as incorrectly identifying something to be the cause of a problem. It is also having an unconscious bias toward accepting new information that supports the views we already have over information that refutes them.[xv]

Both of these errors are so often discovered in human thinking that many experts believe they are a part of how our brains are hardwired, serving a beneficial purpose to us throughout history. They speed up our response time and allow us to survive when time isn't on our side, letting us perform a more careful and thoughtful analysis.

Studies show that people who look out for their own interest, even if it is contradicted by relevant information, may achieve more in life.[xvi] For example, students who are able to tout their achievements more in a college entrance essay may be more likely to receive a scholarship or be accepted into the university. People who inflate their accomplishments in their own mind might increase their motivation and productivity as a result.

On the other hand, these –sometimes deliberate - errors in reasoning don't always lead to beneficial results. They can cause people to make poor decisions because they don't heed warnings about risks. They think something negative isn't likely to happen to them, or they have convinced themselves that they are better than others around them. They may contribute to bias and stereotypes that already exist within people and make them even more entrenched.

Cognitive illusions can cause people to cling even more tightly to their current beliefs and make them less receptive to information that differs from those beliefs and less willing to listen to people with other viewpoints.

Cognitive biases

We need to be aware that others will seek to use our cognitive illusions to their benefit often without us even realizing it. Salespeople and marketing executives know just the right words to use and images to display to capitalize on our cognitive biases and increase the likelihood that we will buy their products. Politicians are adept at selecting the perfect images and words in their commercials to take advantage of the fears of voters when it comes to an economic downturn, levels of crime, changes in gun laws, detrimental effects of climate change, or concerns over immigrants crossing the border. They might use ominous music or a certain tone of voice to help stoke the fears of their constituents and increase the likelihood that they will vote for them in the election.

Are we good judges of ourselves and our abilities? Probably not. Thomas Gilovich, a psychology professor at Cornell University, conducted a survey of one million high school seniors. In this survey, seventy percent of the participants identified themselves as having leadership skills that were above average while only two percent thought their skills were below average. Obviously it is statistically impossible for such a large percentage of people to be above average, but this naiveté isn't limited to the young. Other studies have shown that ninety-four percent of college professors believe that they perform better than their colleagues and most people identify themselves as above average in nearly every area of their life from how lucky they are to their ability to be open-minded and everything in between. Most people also think they are less likely than others to make mistakes in their thinking, which we know isn't exactly the truth.[xvii]

Belief Bias

Belief bias is a common cognitive illusion that occurs when we have a gut instinct that a conclusion reached makes sense and is correct instead of using our critical thinking skills to objectively analyze the information before us.

Jonathan Evans, Julie Barston, and Paul Pollard conducted a study in which people were presented a list of syllogisms and asked to evaluate them.[xviii] A syllogism is an argument composed of two assumptions and a conclusion. The conclusion is supposed to be logically drawn from the assumptions. The researchers were trying to determine how likely people are to just accept ideas at face value that fit in with their existing beliefs instead of taking the time to critically examine their validity.

Take a moment to look at my examples of syllogisms. Consider whether the conclusion I draw from the assumptions is valid or invalid.

Most birds fly in the air. An ostrich is a bird. Therefore, an ostrich flies in the air.
All fish have gills. An octopus has gills. Therefore, an octopus is a fish.
Colorful snakes are venomous. A king snake is colorful. A king snake is venomous.

My first syllogism is not valid. The word *most* is the key. It lets you know that not all birds fly. Some birds that do not fly are ostriches, kiwis, and emus.

The second conclusion is also not valid. While it is true that all fish have gills, that does not mean that all animals with gills have to be fish. An octopus is a mollusk and crustaceans also breathe with gills. Most amphibians have gills and lungs because they spend part of their lives in the water and part on land.

The third syllogism is a little trickier. It is true that many snakes with patterns and bright colors are venomous. If my first assumption had said all colorful snakes are venomous, the argument would have been valid even though the conclusion would be false. But I did not include the word all. You may have inferred that I meant all colorful snakes are not venomous, but it was not stated so a common sense approach would be to read the first assumption as "Many colorful snakes are venomous." That makes the argument invalid because there is not enough information given to determine if the specific king snake is venomous.

Confirmation Bias

Confirmation bias is our tendency to accept information as true if it supports the beliefs we already hold and to ignore or dismiss information that disputes our views. Everyone is susceptible to this cognitive bias and must be on guard against it. Even the greatest minds may become so attached to a theory they hold that if they conduct an argument that has results that seem to disagree with the theory, they are more likely to question the importance of the argument points than they are to question or abandon the theory.[xix]

Why is confirmation bias so prevalent in our thinking? Because we are often overconfident in our abilities to make correct decisions and judgments.

For example, if an employer thinks a potential job candidate is a good fit for a position after an interview, they are more likely to pay attention to items on their resume or from their references that support their opinion while information that does not. This may or may not work out in the employer's favor.

Similarly, a basketball coach who feels that players over six feet tall perform the best athletically is likely to mostly recruit players of that height. This may cause them to miss out on some other very talented players as well.

<u>Hindsight bias</u>
Hindsight bias is taking credit for "knowing something all along" and being able to predict it before it happened. The downfall with this bias is that we put all of the emphasis on the outcome and none on the decision making or process that went into it. This often leads to us giving decision makers too much credit or blame for the result instead of objectively assessing everyone's contribution and the quality of the decisions that were made.

Egocentric Bias

This bias occurs when people think so highly of themselves and their abilities that it keeps them from looking at information and situations objectively. There are two main types of this bias:

- Argument from authority is when someone thinks they know more than others around them so they are overly confident that their opinion must be correct.
- An ad hominem, Latin for "against the man," argument is when someone avoids the substance of the argument by attacking the morality, character, judgment, or some other personal aspect about the other party.

Key Points
- Critical thinking does not come easily or naturally. It involves making a conscious choice to practice and strengthen your ability to ask questions. It doesn't have to be formal. Critical thinking helps you to make informed,

objective decisions in the real world on a regular basis.

- Everyone brings with them cognitive biases that they often are not aware of. There is no escaping them. Strong critical thinkers increase their awareness of their own personal biases and their ability to recognize the biases of others in order to overcome them and gain the best possible information available to them.

- Cognitive biases wouldn't exist, much less be hardwired in our brains, if they didn't serve some purpose in our lives and aid in our survival. We just need to be aware of them and keep them in check to not sabotage our life today, which is different than the life of hunter-gatherers of the past

Chapter 3: How Are Our Thoughts Influenced?

Take a moment to clear your thoughts. Just sit quietly and think for a few minutes about something you're certain you like. Take a deep breath and close your eyes if that helps. What were you thinking about? Were you thinking with your head or your heart? Chances are you were thinking with your emotions more than with the logical and rational reasoning side of your brain. Often what we are thinking is actually what we are feeling. If you become aware of this part of your cognitive processing, you can better steer yourself back toward the rational process of thought.

Whether we make choices in order to fit in with the crowd, follow the experts, emulate people we admire, or achieve things we want and that we see others have, quite often our thoughts are not our own, but are influenced largely by outside social forces. From what we wear, to where we go on vacation, to our opinions about politics and current events, to the type of house we want to live in or car we want to drive, to what diet we choose to follow and everything in between, so many of our thoughts are influenced by others, often in ways we don't even recognize.

Consumer demands in the 21st century's hardly ever represent human needs in the most literal sense. The demand is rather formed and changed by fashionable products and activities dictated by contemporary influencers. Who are they? If you use LinkedIn, you've probably received emails about the opinions and view of their selected "top influencers" in business related industries. Instagram also has its set of influencers, generally in fashion, travel, pets, and sports categories. These people have lots of followers. When I say lots, I mean several hundred thousand or even millions. When someone's posts are seen by so many people, that must mean they are important and know something very well, right? This is when our irrational thinking kicks in and we are vulnerable to the bandwagon effect and halo effect, and we start queuing behind the other two million to try to become a little bit more like the influencer.

Today it is even harder to keep our emulation of the Joneses in check because now we also have to battle well-directed computer algorithms that remember our browsing history as we shop online for our favorite items. Before we know it, we'll see these or similar items all over our social media platforms because "based on your browsing history, we thought you might like this." We are trapped. It's not enough that ads encourage our existing wants. Their main goal is to create new wants in us, and then again new wants for us to purchase. The options we have seem to be unlimited. Then one day you wake up owning 365 of the same item in different colors or patterns because you routinely fell prey to the cognitive bias created by social media influencers and calculated marketing, targeting your specific wants.

Indoctrination

One of the many purposes of critical thinking is to allow people to analyze information from all sides and viewpoints, to challenge and question that information, to become certain it is accurate, to objectively make an informed decision, gather deeper knowledge and understanding, come up with answers or the best possible solution, uncover the truth, and adapt or abandon their currently held beliefs if evidence warrants it. Indoctrination is the opposite of all of that. Indoctrination teaches ideas from only one point of view and expects them to be accepted completely without being questioned or challenged.

We teach our children about what is right and wrong at an early age because we know that they will inevitably be faced with moral and ethical dilemmas throughout their entire lives. But teaching them the difference between right and wrong is simply not enough. If we don't also teach them critical thinking skills that can be practiced, developed, and strengthened, we are doing them an extreme disservice. Instead of being able to form their own rational moral judgments throughout their lives, they may fall victim to propaganda and indoctrination from sources that do not necessarily share truth or have their best interest at heart. That danger is not just reserved for children. Anyone who lacks critical judgment is at risk.

Ethics and morals are not something that is easy to teach as one might think. The world doesn't work in black and white absolutes. There are many shades of gray in between. People often assume that the beliefs and values that they hold about what is morally right and wrong are correct and constant, but they will inevitably be faced with situations in their lives when the line between right and wrong becomes a little less clear. Consider the belief that it is always wrong to take another human life. At face value most of us would hopefully agree with that, but there are plenty of gray areas even there. What if someone killed a person attempting to kill them? What about a patient who was suffering terribly and had no chance of recovery ends his or her own life? We tend to think that our morals and values are universal and correct in all situations, but that is seldom the case. There are many different cultures in the world that may hold beliefs that are different from our own, but that doesn't make any of them more or less correct.

Life is complicated, and that's what makes having strong critical thinking skills all the more important. Critical thinking encourages people to hear and accept information from more than one perspective in an effortto produce educated, open-minded, and well informed citizens. Thus they can question the information presented to them and make sound judgments and decisions for themselves. Critical thinking allows us to take our power back and reclaim our thinking and beliefs as our own.

Propaganda operates with the help of two other key features, which are prejudice and public relations. Collectively they are referred as the three Ps. Today we associate the concept of propaganda with brainwashing, and manipulation – something we see as negative.

The word propaganda, before the Nazis' hate-spreading, political movement, held a different connotation. Pre-modern propaganda dates back to 515 BCE. Most historians agree that the Behistun Inscription in Persia (today Iran) can be considered one of the first examples of propaganda in the world. The Behistun Inscription describes the rise of Darius I to the Persian throne.[xx] Propaganda was used in a religious context to spread Catholicism to non-Catholic countries back in the 1600s, and also to spread the Reformation as an alternative view on the Christian religion.[xxi] By the mid 1800s it was already being used in politics and had earned its negative meaning. Evidence shows that it was used in Rome after Caesar's death when Octavian and Mark Antony were fighting for control Rome, in the American Revolutions amongst the Patriots;[xxii] and in the Russian "October Revolution" in 1917.[xxiii] I personally love the Howard Chandler Christy WWI military recruitment posters commissioned by the US government. All these propaganda associations existed well before the Third Reich.

In the following section I will present how the meaning of the word "propaganda" changed with the spreading of Nazism and what were the key "success" formulas Hitler used to gain his massive support basis. The Nazis used propaganda incredibly well; probably better than it ever has been done before or ever since. Fear and propaganda were well run machines in the Third Reich. Hitler came into Germany at a time when the country was terribly economically depressed because they were still paying war reparations for WWI. The National Socialist German Workers Party took advantage of the state of a very beaten down group of people and told them it was the fault of the Jews, who had stolen all their wealth and caused all their problems.

Leni Reifenstahl directed one of the key pieces of Hitler's propaganda - *Triumph of the Will*. She used new and innovative camera techniques. When you watch it, the young, robust German boys and men are shown are compared to the old hunched Jewish men with hooked noses and wrinkles and moles.[xxiv] This was in 1934, but the video was so iconic in what it did for Hitler, that it basically destroyed Riefenstahl's career after the war because of the impact and influence it had.

While the ideology spread was one of the most despicable ones in human history, Hitler and his right-hand man, Joseph Goebbels, certainly knew how to use propaganda to it's fullest potential. Important lessons can be learned by critically analyzing their system of persuasion. These lessons can serve a good purpose of knowing how propaganda indoctrinates individuals on a mass scale and how to apply critical thinking skills to avoid political, religious, or hate propaganda today.

Dark lessons from Nazism

The literal definition of the concept of propaganda, planting ideas, is not inherently good or bad What determines whether sharing information with others is beneficial or harmful is dependent on what information you are spreading, how and why you are spreading it, and how will it impact others. The ways that Hitler used propaganda to plant hateful ideas in the minds of his followers and indoctrinate them forever changed the connotation we have for the word propaganda and enforced again and again how important a free and independent press, freedom of speech, and critical thinking really are.

Hitler and his allies were very good at mass-suggestion and playing on people's emotions in order to manipulate them and persuade them to believe their message. Hitler understood that an argument firmly based on evidence has much less of an impact on influencing popular opinion than stirring up strong emotions.

In his book, *Mein Kampf*, Hitler wrote of the importance of knowing the feelings of the people so you could capitalize on them, capture their attention, and get your message across to them in such a way that they would understand it and be motivated to follow it. He further went on to point out that as a whole, people aren't very intelligent, and they quickly forgot what you told them, so the propaganda you spread should be kept to just a few key ideas and repeated as a slogan over and over to increase the likelihood that they would remember your message and follow what you want them to do. Repetition of short, memorable slogans was key in the marketing of his message. "The receptivity of great masses is very limited, their intelligence is small, but their power of forgetting is enormous. (…) all effective propaganda must be limited to a very few points and must harp on these in slogans."[xxv]

Despite his disdain for the masses, Hitler knew that playing on their feelings rather than their intellect would work to his benefit. He was able to come across as likeable and charming. While his message wasn't always instantly welcomed, Hitler was a bit like a snake charmer in that he could really captivate an audience and command their attention so that they would want to follow him and fully support his message. Hitler's ability to assess how the common people were feeling and tailor the delivery of his message so he could market it and enabled the Nazis to quickly move from being a small group of discontented ex-military to a movement with millions of followers.

We are often thinking what we are feeling.[xxvi] Hitler knew this very well. In the following paragraphs I will present how he used emotional responses to annihilate the rational part of the brain. For critical thinkers, this is a crucial technique to be aware of. Familiarity with this type of brainwashing will help recognize it quickly so one can return to rational arguments instead of acting on distorted emotions.

Hitler's goal was to capture the attention of the masses, but he also wanted to avoid any debates. He was controlling the information that people could access. He knew his audience inside out, understood their motivations, fears, sensitivities, and was not shy to trigger the emotions related to these pain points.

He separated his possible audience as falling into one of three groups:

• People who believed everything they read. This is the largest group and is composed of people who are gullible and easily persuaded. They are the proverbial sheep.

• People who no longer believed in anything. This group used to believe everything they read, but something happened to upset them and they became disenchanted and distrustful of all news outlets. They either avoided reading the papers at all or completely distrusted and questioned them. They were suspicious to the core. In Hitler's opinion, this group was hard to handle, thus useless for political purposes.

- People who are critical thinkers and made judgments of their own based on an objective and thoughtful examination of facts and evidence. Hitler thought highly of this group saying, "the importance of these splendid people lies only in their intelligence not in their number."[xxvii]

Hitler knew that he needed numbers and assessed that the numbers were in his favor if he could manipulate the first group, the masses. People who were easily persuaded and believed everything they read made up a larger percentage of the population than the others even today. This is a universal truth. It was true in the mid-nineteen hundreds; it will be true forever.

The other two groups would have split opinions, so Hitler targeted the more gullible group, and believed if he could control education and the press, there would be no stopping him. Sadly, his assumptions were largely correct.

The power in Hitler's message laid in his packaging. Most of his infamous book, *Mein Kampf*, consists of oratorical ideas; descriptions of peoples' appearances (focusing on their differences, especially between the Germans and the Jews); and irrelevant, but emotionally charged, stories. He carefully avoided engaging in intellectual reasoning and debates.

The foundation of the Nazi platform was rooted firmly in prejudice. This may not seem surprising when one considers the hateful message that reached their millions of followers and ultimately lead to such unimaginable human tragedy. The terrifying secret behind the "success" of prejudice is that it's deeply engrained in the human psyche. Whether it is people of a different race, religion, gender, physical or mental ability, socioeconomic status, culture, country, or even age group, it seems that humans can find a limitless supply of reasons to be prejudiced against people who are different from them.

Hitler recognized this human gullibility, and to fully appeal to it, he tried to cite scientific facts as a basis for his message. He used Herbert Spencer's modified version of Darwin's theory of evolution called Social Darwinism to prove his ideas on German superiority.

Social Darwinism, originating from the writings of Herbert Spencer, stated that human societies developed like natural organisms. The idea of the struggle for survival was also mentioned in his work. Spencer suggested that this struggle brought an inevitable progress in society. The term 'survival of the fittest' also comes from Spencer's work. The ideas presented in Social Darwinism led Hitler to label many groups as being inferior to Germans and the need for pure blood Germans to avoid mating with people in those groups in order for them to "maintain their superiority and dominance." He wanted to create an ideal state in which all inferior people had been eliminated. In *Mein Kampf* he wrote, "Whoever would live, let him fight, and he who does not want to do battle in this world of eternal struggle, does not deserve life." From here it was not a huge leap to call the Russian invasion the German's "struggle for survival" and the genocide of the Jews the "defence against Jewish communism." Social Darwinism gave a scientific coating to a rabid psychotic belief.[xxviii]

Using scientific evidence as a crutch to prop up an argument or message and give it an air of credibility is not a new idea. It did not begin and end with the Nazis; it was used during the time of Plato and is still used today even in some of the most developed countries of the world. Let's take the propagandist movement that lead to the scheduling of narcotic drugs such as marijuana, cocaine, heroin, etc. Many of those were legal substances bought readily over the counter at a pharmacy in the early 1900s.

In the 1910s, because of the Mexican Revolution, many Mexicans immigrated to the U.S. They had their own uses for cannabis, calling it "marihuana." Besides medicinal purposes, they also smoked it recreationally. This was an unknown practice for white Americans. Politicians quickly took advantage of this knowledge-practice gap to label cannabis "marihuana" to make it sound Mexican. And at that time, Mexican meant bad. In the 1920s, anti-marijuana campaigns specifically aimed to raise awareness about the harmful effects of the substance. The questionable scientific "evidence," in these campaigns made claims such as marijuana turned users into killers and drug addicts. In reality the campaigns were an attempt to get rid of Mexican immigrants. Later the drug-user label was spread to a larger group of people, including black people, Filipinos, and entertainers in general.[xxix] Eventually marijuana and other previously available drugs became Schedule I narcotics whether or not the label was warranted.[xxx]

Trying to use science to give credence to a viewpoint that is blatant prejudice is a bit like trying to put lipstick on a pig. You can try to dress up the argument, but at its core it remains the same. The important lesson for critical thinkers is to be aware and spot when people try to disguise prejudice behind a mask of science. I always taught my children to double-check scientific evidence, triple check statements without any evidence, and to look at the other side of the argument. Things are rarely black or white, but beware of endorsing gray areas without taking the time to properly research them yourself.

Spot the Persuasion Techniques Used on You

If you went through the day with your eyes and ears open, you'd find yourself surrounded by media inundating you with messages. In fact, if you watch an hour long television show anywhere from fourteen to sixteen minutes of your time will be spent watching commercials. Everywhere you turn messages in media are trying to persuade you to believe, buy, or do something.

These messages have a language all their own. They have such a limited amount of time to grab your attention and communicate with you that every single word is chosen with deliberate care. They do not select neutral or random words. Nothing is left to chance when it comes to how they want you to receive and interpret their messages and information.

Advertisers try to persuade you to buy their product or a service they offer. Public relations experts try to "sell" you an image: a positive view of a candidate, company, or organization. Campaigning or advocacy groups try to persuade you to buy into certain beliefs, values, issues, policies, or a specific candidate by painting their opinion and viewpoint as being factual in order to get you to believe what they say in debates and elect them to political office or to pass their amendment. [xxxi]

No matter which of those groups are involved, they all use specific language to persuade us. Advertisers and public relations experts tend to link a product or candidate with something that their target audience is known to already think of favorably and like.

For example, Tom Selleck and Alex Trebek are popular celebrity figures, especially to those in older generations. It is not surprising to see them hired by advertisers to inspire trust in such products as reverse home mortgages and life insurance policies in which the target audience is people in those age groups. Nike, on the other hand, targets the younger generations so they bring in popular athletes who appeal to younger age groups for their advertising campaigns like Colin Kaepernick and Lebron James. When it comes to creating a positive image for a candidate running for office, you are likely to see commercials depicting them as involved in their community or as very committed and close to their families.

There are campaign and advocacy groups who often create a negative picture of an opposing candidate or viewpoint and evoke a feeling of anger or fear in the people who see their advertisements and persuade them to vote for the candidate they support. You see negative political ads all the time, depicting an opposing candidate as being soft on crime, showing images designed to cause fear in people who view them. If the goal is to persuade people that a candidate doesn't care about the environment, they will show images of factories polluting the air, water filled with sludge or oil, and sick animals. They focus on associating a candidate or political issue with something that they believe their target voters don't like and evokes a strong emotional response from them.

The horror stories depicted in ads are often exaggerated or even irrelevant to people's lives, but they create a strong and lasting emotional transfer in their target audience through their use of implied association.

Those who are savvy in their marketing skills know their target audience well and are adept at tailoring their message in such a way that it will be extremely persuasive to them. We are exposed to this multiple times a day, and we may not even be aware it's happening. There are six common techniques that are used by those who wish to persuade us. We should become more aware of and keep an eye out for the following tricks:

- *Going along with the crowd.* This trick plays on our human tendency to want to fit in with the group. Psychology calls this cognitive bias the bandwagon effect. This technique depicts a product or service as making large groups of people happy or improving their lives. Naturally, we would want that for ourselves too. Let's take a restaurant as an example. If certain people often endorse the food served there, especially people we feel strongly about like our closest friends, our favorite TV stars, or even trustworthy grandmas, we might feel tempted to try it even if normally that restaurant wouldn't be our primary choice.

- *Live up to a high standard of success.* This technique capitalizes on our desire to be like our role models or people we look up to.

Marketers use celebrities, attractive people, and those portrayed as wealthy or successful because they know we want to achieve the things in our lives that we assume they already have. Their challenge is to convince us that those things are reasonably within our reach to attain.

- *"Trust me, I'm an expert."* Human nature is to put a high value on the opinions of people we consider to be experts. This is why many people in commercials are dressed as doctors, dentists, scientists, police officers, teachers, and other professionals. Logically, we may understand that they are really actors paid to appear in a commercial, but the visual portrayal of them as an expert in the area they are speaking about can be a powerful, persuasive tool.

- *Talking a lot, saying very little.* We may think that a company, candidate, or expert is making a bold and outrageous statement or stand when in reality they are actually saying very little. They can get by with making unsubstantiated, exaggerated, and even false claims by inserting words like may, could, some, many, or can, which provide them cover from being accused of lying.

- In the words of Mae West, *"Flattery will get you everywhere."* People skilled in marketing understand that everyone likes to be flattered, so they go out of their way to make their target audience feel important and that they value their opinions, purchasing decisions, and wise judgment.

- *That loving feeling.* Marketing experts like to include images of things people love, enjoy, and find comforting when possible because they create positive feelings in the people they want to reach. It might be cute animals, loving families celebrating the holidays together, curling up by the fire with a warm blanket and a read book, or strolling along the beach at sunset. The point is if your audience is happy, they will be more likely to associate those good feelings with your candidate, product, service, or message.

- *Scientific evidence.* This is the particular technique where marketers strengthen their message with science. They use charts, graphs, and statistics that the average Joe doesn't even understand to prove their product is legit. This is an effective persuasion method because many people trust science and scientists. Don't fall for everything. Look closely at the evidence, because it's quite often misleading.

- *Simple solution.* Our life is so complicated, we are so complex, our problems are so hard to solve... But XYZ company has a unique, simple solution to all of these issues. Isn't that nice to hear? Of course it is. Persuaders know this so they often offer help by proposing a simple solution. Advertisers take this strategy as far as suggesting that a car, a brand, or a cleaning product will make you desirable, popular, a good mom, and successful.[xxxii]

Key Points

• While Adolf Hitler was a horrible person who espoused a message of hatred to his followers, we can learn a lot from how he marketed his message in a way that resonated so strongly with his target audience.

• Indoctrination is only allowing people to receive information from one source or viewpoint with the expectation that it will be accepted completely without question or challenge. Critical thinking is the cure for that.

•   Many of our thoughts are not our own. They stem from our emotions and allow us to be easily influenced by others if we aren't careful. Critical thinkers are aware of this and make conscious efforts to resist the pull of their emotions in favor of a more objective and rational approach.

•   Everywhere we turn, we are inundated with messages trying to persuade us to think, vote, and act in certain ways. As critical thinkers, we should be aware of the language and persuasive techniques that are at work attempting to influence us each day so that we can make the best and most informed decisions for ourselves.

Chapter 4: Learning Models for Critical Thinking

Bloom's Taxonomy

Educational psychologist, Dr. Benjamin Bloom, thought there should be much more to education than just repetition, drill, memorization, and rote learning. In 1956 he created a system that we refer to as Bloom's taxonomy, which was designed to encourage higher level critical thinking in students. With some modification over time, Bloom's work is still valued and used in our schools today.

Bloom's taxonomy is visually shaped as a triangle, moving through six levels, with knowledge serving as the base at the bottom.

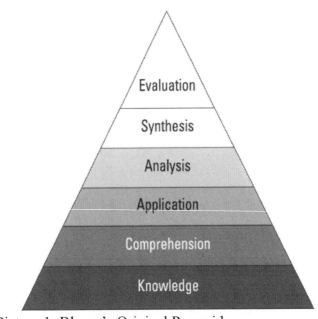

Picture 1: Bloom's Original Pyramid.

1. Level 1 – Knowledge: Bloom considered knowledge to be the most basic level of thought. He defined it as recalling information previously learned. For a critical thinker, this would be simply remembering data and information he had seen, heard, or read before.

2. Level 2 – Comprehension: This is a step up from knowledge as it requires people

to understand the meaning of information they have learned. At this level of thinking, you might compare and contrast information you received from different sources or predict what would happen in the future based on current and past performance and behavior.

3. Level 3 – Application: This level requires thinkers to take the information they have learned and use it in new situations. Critical thinkers working at the application level can take facts they have learned and use them to make new arguments and raise new questions.

4. Level 4 – Analysis: At this level a robust understanding of the information learned is needed. For critical thinkers, analysis may mean taking the arguments of others and breaking them down into smaller

parts in order to better understand and examine them for possible errors in reasoning.

5. Level 5 – Synthesis: This level involves putting information together in order to create something new. Synthesis usually follows analysis because analysis is about taking data apart and examining the parts in isolation, looking for differences. Synthesis is putting the parts back together, looking for similarities and connection between these parts.

6. Level 6- Evaluation: This is the highest level of thinking located at the top of the triangle of Bloom's taxonomy. This level builds upon all of the knowledge and information gained and created from all of the lower levels and judges its merit and value. This is what critical thinkers do

once they have completed their research, thoroughly examined it for possible errors in reasoning, created new arguments, and are now ready to make judgments and decisions of their own.

Lower order thinking skills

Lower order thinking skills include knowledge, comprehension, and application on Bloom's pyramid. Activities that need these kinds of thinking skills will require the thinker to recite information, and facts, and organize them to solve problems. Verbs connected to lower order thinking skills are recall, choose, find, define, demonstrate, explain, build, develop, and utilize.

Higher order thinking skills

Higher order thinking skills require analysis, synthesis, and evaluation. Cognitive skills of this level allow the person to categorize, classify, compare and contrast information it in order to make a decision. Verbs of higher order thinking include: combine, create, design, develop, evaluate, justify, and measure.

Critical thinking skills

Good critical thinking skills need both higher and lower order thinking as defined by Bloom. Critical thinking can be divided into two skill sections: 1) skills to collect and create information (lower order thinking) and 2) using those skills to guide behavior (higher order thinking). Thinking critically about something with the purpose of making an informed decision requires the thinker to go through each level of Bloom's pyramid: knowledge, comprehension, application, analysis, synthesis, and evaluation. Important decisions that are made without going through these stages may not be the best ones and may bring undesired results.[xxxiii]

In the 1990s, a group of cognitive psychologists including one of Bloom's former students, Lorin Anderson, made some revisions and updates to the triangle. Their six levels of thinking are: Remembering, Understanding, Applying, Analyzing, Evaluating, and Creating.

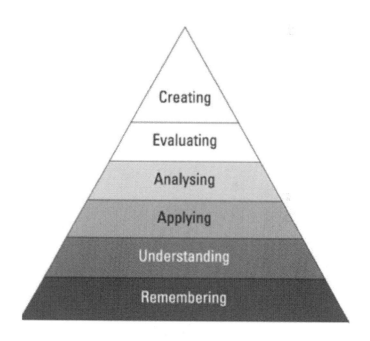

Picture 2: Bloom's Triangle Revised by Lorin Anderson

While the levels arguably hold the same meaning as in the previous version of the triangle, the terminologies being only reframed from nouns to verbs, Anderson added a second dimension to the taxonomy. He outlined a knowledge dimension next to the cognitive processing dimension, defining what kind of knowledge can be learned (factual, conceptual, procedural, and meta-cognitive). Find the revised two-dimensional taxonomy in Picture 3:[xxxiv]

Bloom's Taxonomy							
	The Cognitive Process Dimension						
The Knowledge Dimension	Remember	Understand	Apply	Analyze	Evaluate	Create	
Factual Knowledge	List	Summarize	Classify	Order	Rank	Combine	
Conceptual Knowledge	Describe	Interpret	Experiment	Explain	Assess	Plan	
Procedural Knowledge	Tabulate	Predict	Calculate	Differentiate	Conclude	Compose	
Meta-Cognitive Knowledge	Appropriate Use	Execute	Construct	Achieve	Action	Actualize	

Picture 3: The Second Dimension of Bloom's Taxonomy. *Downloaded from*

http://projects.coe.uga.edu/epltt/

Bloom's Taxonomy has faced criticism over the years as well. Some questioned how rigorously and systematically it was constructed. Other critics acknowledge the six levels of thinking that Bloom identified, but cautions against overstating the hierarchal connections between them. They are concerned that sometimes teachers see the lower levels on the triangle as being unimportant and may not teach or develop them in their students. They stress that those lower levels are critical to practice and establish before higher levels of thinking can take place. Another criticism is that thinking is so interconnected that it is impossible to separate it into categories as often many of them occur at the same time.[xxxv][xxxvi]

Despite any criticism of Bloom's taxonomy, there is no question of the important role it has played and continues to play in education. It shined a light on the need to develop higher level thinking skills in children and provided teachers with a guide and framework for doing so. It added rigor and depth to the ways students were taught and asked to demonstrate their knowledge and understanding of what they had learned.

Perhaps, most importantly, it showed us that teaching our children content is simply not enough. We must also equip them with the skills they need to reason and think for themselves.

The SOLO Taxonomy

Bloom's taxonomy has also inspired other new models to be created, including one by two Australians, psychologist and author John Biggs and business consultant Kevin Collis, called the Structure of Observed Learning Outcome taxonomy, or SOLO taxonomy, which identifies five levels of thought:

- Pre-structural: people don't yet understand the topic.

- Uni-structural: people have a very basic knowledge of the topic but only in one area.

- Multi-structural: people know that there are several different components to the topic, but they don't see the connections between them.

- Relational: learners can now understand the interconnectedness of ideas within the topic. This is the highest level that most people reach in their thinking on a given concept.

- Extended Abstract: some people are able to reach this pinnacle level of thought by taking their complete understanding of a concept and stretching it to create a new idea.[xxxvii]

Bloom's Taxonomy versus SOLO Taxonomy

Scientists in the field of education argue that Biggs and Collis' taxonomy is much better structured and more applicable to actual learning and thinking than Bloom's model. I collected a few arguments that support this statement.[xxxviii][xxxix]

The SOLO taxonomy is based on the real, researched structure of student learning outcomes. Bloom developed his taxonomy from proposal by educator committees. SOLO presents the theory of teaching and learning. Bloom's taxonomy is the theory of knowledge.

The SOLO levels are easier to communicate and has multiple ways in which it can be communicated like written form, hand signs, and symbols. Bloom's taxonomy can be only communicated through writing.

The SOLO method is simple, so it can be used to educate children as young as five to look at their own learning outcomes. Finally, SOLO is a model that inspires trust in students, showing that learning is the result of effort and strategies, not just talent, or ability.[xl]

Paul-Elder Critical Thinking Framework

Dr. Richard Paul, the Director of Research and Professional Development at the Center for Critical Thinking and former Chair of the National Council for Excellence in Critical Thinking, wrote numerous books and articles on the subject that garnered him world recognition. He worked with his wife, Dr. Linda Elder, an educational psychologist, author, teacher, and presenter, who is also recognized as an authority on critical thinking. She is the president of the Foundation for Critical Thinking as well as the executive director of the Center for Critical Thinking. The Paul-Elder framework is composed by three parts:

- The elements of thought (reasoning),
- The intellectual standards that should be applied to the elements of reasoning;
- The intellectual traits associated with a cultivated critical thinker that result from the consistent and disciplined application of the

intellectual standards to the elements of thought."^xli

According to Paul and Elder, to upgrade thinking, one needs to be able to identify the parts of their thinking and then to assess their use of these parts of thinking.

The eight elements of thought (reasoning):

1. **Purpose:**

    "All reasoning has a purpose."

    Behind any reasoning there is always a purpose which must be considered. The purpose is the goal you are trying to achieve with the reasoning. You might want to solve a problem, answer a question, or increase understanding, but you must know where you are going or you will never know when you get there. Be sure to check in with your purpose frequently to ensure you are still conveying the desired message.

2. **Question**

   "All reasoning is an attempt to figure something out, to settle some question, to solve some problem."

   The question will guide your thinking to answers, so it must be very clear and precise. It will be the driving force as you seek information, thus it has to be worded carefully. You can break the overarching question down into smaller, more manageable underlying questions if it helps to maintain your focus and direction.

3. **Assumptions**

   "All reasoning is based on assumptions."

   Assumptions are the beliefs you hold that don't require much thought. They may even be kept in your subconscious. Recognize how your assumptions have a major impact on the way you view the world. You should periodically assess your beliefs to make sure they are supported by evidence.

4. **Point of View**

   "All reasoning is done from some point of view."

   Avoid assuming your point of view is the only one or it is more important than others. The way one sees the world is only one lens through which he or she can view it. Be fair when analyzing opinions that are different from yours.

5. **Information**

   "All reasoning is based on data, information, and evidence."

   The information that you try to gather to answer a question or solve a problem needs to be accurate, relevant, and backed up by facts and evidence. You will need to make sure your personal cognitive biases and opinions don't distort the way you evaluate information. Objectivity and open-mindedness are crucial to gathering evidence that both supports and disputes your ideas for analysis.

6. **Inferences**

"All reasoning contains inferences or interpretations by which we draw conclusions and give meaning to data."

Inferences are the conclusions your mind reaches as it tries to make sense of the information presented to it. Your inferences need to be based on the facts of the evidence you find. They should make logical sense and consistent with each other.

7. **Concepts**

    "All reasoning is expressed through, and shaped by, concepts and ideas."

    Concepts are the ideas and theories you generate as you try to make sense of what is going on in the world around you. You need to understand the ideas and theories you give prominence in your life and make sure that you have justification for them. Be certain that you have explored alternative explanations and you can clearly explain your ideas and concepts.

8. **Implications and Consequences**

    "All reasoning leads somewhere or has implications and consequences."

    Implications arise from your thoughts. Critical thinkers consider the implications of their thoughts before they plan a course of action. Consequences arise from your actions. You should think through what might happen if you make a decision to act and what could happen if you decide not to act. Consider all possible implications and consequences and recognize that not all of them will be positive.[xlii]

The Intellectual Standards

In Paul and Elder's framework, the intellectual standards are used to assess the quality of reasoning. Aspiring critical thinkers need to have a good knowledge of these standards. The main goal of the intellectual standards is to help the individual become infused in all thinking and become better at reasoning.

- Accuracy: When you are trying to determine the accuracy of information, you might ask:
    - How could we verify that?
    - How could we find out if that is true?
    - Do any other sources support those findings?

- Precision: When you are trying to increase precision, you may ask:
    - Can you be more specific?
    - Can you be more detailed in your description?
    - Could you be more exact?

- Relevance: When you are trying to determine the relevance of a piece of information, you may ask:
    - How is that connected to the problem at hand?
    - How does it help us solve the problem?
    - How does that bear on the question?

- Depth: When you are trying to determine the depth of information, you might ask:
    - What makes this challenging?

- What are some difficulties we are going to have to overcome?
- What are some of the complexities of this question?

- Breadth: When addressing the breadth of information, you may need to consider:
  - Do we need to consider any other points of view?
  - Are there any other ways we can look at this?
  - Do we need to look at this from another perspective?

- Logic: When you need to see if the information is logical, you may ask:
  - Does this information make sense?
  - Does this go along with the evidence and fit into the bigger picture?
  - Does your first paragraph fit in with your last one?

- Significance: When considering the significance of information, you might ask:
    - Is this the most important thing we should think about?
    - What is the most important idea for us to address?
    - Which of these facts are most important?

- Fairness: To ensure fairness, you want to consider:
    - Have all perspectives been heard and represented?
    - Are any of the facts being altered to support certain opinions over others?
    - Is my thinking justifiable in this context?
    - Is my purpose fair given the situation?

Intellectual Traits

If you apply the intellectual standards consistently in your thinking, you'll develop some intellectual traits. The traits identified by Paul and Elder are the following:

- Intellectual Humility

Intellectual humility involves recognizing the possession of cognitive and personal biases. It is being willing to work to overcome those biases in order to be more objective and make informed decisions. People who display intellectual humility are more likely to be receptive to learning from others who think differently from themselves. They tend to be liked and respected by others because they openly value what others bring to the table.

Intellectually humble people want to learn more and are open to finding information from a variety of sources.

- Intellectual Courage

People who demonstrate intellectual courage are willing to take risks if it means they will learn the truth in the end. They are not refusing to back away from beliefs and viewpoints they have strong negative feelings about. They are willing to face them and listen with an open mind before passing judgment on others.

- Intellectual Empathy

People who are intellectually empathetic are willing to accept that there are people with different viewpoints from their own, but those viewpoints are no less important. Intellectual empathy means that one may have to accept being wrong, even when one was previously sure they were right, especially when evidence proves it.

- Intellectual Autonomy

Intellectual autonomy is taking ownership of and accepting responsibility for one's own thinking. People who are intellectually autonomous do not just passively accept the beliefs of others, but rather look for evidence and make judgments for themselves in a given matter. They do not give into social pressure and do not just go along with the crowd.

- Intellectual Integrity

Intellectual integrity is when someone is true to his own thinking and consistently applies the same critical thinking skills to all of the information he analyzes, displaying intellectual integrity. People should hold everyone—friend, competitor, and oneself—to the same standards proof and evidence to support thoughts and opinions.

- Intellectual Perseverance

People who display the trait of intellectual perseverance don't give up easily on things. They are committed to the long haul to find evidence and make judgments only based on well informed decisions.

- Confidence in Reason

Confidence in reason is the honest belief that in the long run, truth and reason will prevail. It involves believing that people are able to draw evidence-based, well-thought out conclusions by themselves. It is trusting people can become strong, reasonable, rational thinkers over time, and they will ultimately reach conclusions that are good for humanity.

- Fair-mindedness

Fair-mindedness involves giving all viewpoints the same respect and deference. Being fair-minded means considering the perspectives of others and affording them the same value and weight as you do your own, even when they are in clear opposition to your beliefs.

Regular practice of the intellectual traits will help the individual become a sharp, knowledgeable critical thinker. Such a person will be able to raise relevant questions and identify pressing problems while formulating them clearly and accurately. He or she then will gather related information to the questions or problems and interpret this information effectively and contextually. After the assessment of the information is done, the critical thinker will come to a reasonable conclusion and useful solutions. He or she will test the conclusion or solution against relevant standards before applying them, considering possible consequences.[xliii]

Occam's Razor

This critical thinking model is attributed to an English Franciscan friar and theologian, William of Ockham. This model states, "Among competing hypotheses, the one with the fewest assumptions should be selected."[xliv] It is also referred to as the Rule of Simplicity. In scientific fields, simpler theories are favored over complex ones because simple theories are easier to test.

Sir Isaac Newton used Occam's razor as follows: "We are to admit no more causes of natural things than such as are both true and sufficient to explain their appearances. Therefore, to the same natural effects we must, as far as possible, assign the same causes."[xlv]

Occam's Razor also incentivizes people to choose the simplest solution when presented with two equally likely solutions to a problem, "When you hear hoof beats, think horses not zebras."

Inspired by Occam's razor, Robert J. Hanlon made his own razor model that we call Hanlon's razor. His saying, "Never attribute to malice that which is adequately explained by stupidity," suggests a way of eliminating unlikely explanations for human behavior and its consequences.[xlvi]

Key Points:

- Bloom's Taxonomy has had a major impact on education since its creation in 1956. It is also a tool that can benefit critical thinkers in their quest to make objective, informed judgments and decisions.

- Bloom's Taxonomy stresses the importance of learning, practicing, and strengthening higher level thinking skills because simply learning and recalling information is not enough.

- Dr. Richard Paul and Dr. Linda Elder worked together to identify eight elements of thinking they believed people need to master in order to improve their thinking: purpose, question, assumptions, point of view, information, inferences, concepts, and implications and consequences.

- The universal intellectual standards should be utilized anytime you are trying to critically analyze your thinking about a problem or theory, include: clarity, accuracy, precision, relevance, depth, breadth, logic, significance, and fairness.

- Paul and Elder defined a set of valuable intellectual traits they feel all strong critical thinkers should display after practicing the universal intellectual standards rigorously: humility, courage, empathy, autonomy, integrity, perseverance, confidence in reason, and fair-mindedness.

- In scientific fields, simpler theories are favored over complex ones because simple theories are easier to be tested and more likely to be correct.

Chapter 5: Critical Thinking As Dr. Kahneman Knows

This chapter is devoted to discussing the work of American psychologist, Daniel Kahneman. His book, *Thinking Fast and Slow*,[xlvii] has contributed so much to understanding our cognitive biases, thinking pathways, brain functions. Kahneman's guiding belief is that humans are illogical beings who often misjudge situations in predictable patterns.

Our brains are hard-wired to want to respond to situations quickly because throughout history our very survival often depended on it. We crave a quick and easy solution to problems because there were times when making quick decisions has been a matter of life and death. When we feel threatened, our brains switch into "fight or flight" mode as we want to make an immediate decision about how to best protect ourselves. This is what Kahneman refers to as "fast thinking."

But there are times when taking a moment to pause and carefully evaluate the situation in order to come up with a thoughtful plan of action would be much more rational and beneficial. That is "slow thinking," which can be harder to come by.

Dr. Kahneman refers to fast thinking as System 1, "the instant, unconscious, automatic, emotional, intuitive thinking" and slow thinking as System 2, "the slower, conscious, rational, reasoning, deliberate thinking."

Thinking takes a lot of energy! In fact, when we concentrate and think carefully about something, twenty percent of our body's energy is devoted to our brain, which means that energy isn't available to be used for other things. Our brains are designed to want to conserve as much energy as possible, so they try to avoid slow thinking at all costs. Fast thinking is less energy demanding.

For example, when I first got my treadmill, I thought I would be able to multitask and read books as I exercised. It didn't take long to realize if I concentrated on my book, my speed on the treadmill had to slow down. If I kept my speed up, I could read, but I had no idea what I'd just read. My brain and body were not able to do both things simultaneously at the level I wanted.

Intuition and expertise

Our mood has a major impact on our intuition and fast thinking. When we are in a good mood, our intuition is much more accurate than when we are unhappy or uncomfortable. Good mood signals to our brain that things are going smoothly and it's okay to relax a little. It allows us to unleash our creativity, but it can also lead us to make mistakes in reasoning because we are not on high alert. A bad mood, on the other hand, signals that there are problems, and there may be threats ahead so we need to be even more focused, alert, suspicious, and on guard.

Fast thinking has the important job of keeping in check our current view of the world and our sense of what is and isn't normal. But it can be gullible and quick to believe things without questioning them. Without our slow thinking being involved, we can't think critically. With fast thinking, we don't challenge and question the information we receive. With slow thinking, we can practice critical judgment, but as we learned earlier, it's expensive in energy currency.

Fast thinking automatically tries to believe everything. In order to understand what we hear or read, first we make an attempt to see if we believe it. "What would this statement mean if it were true?" we ask ourselves subconsciously. Only when we find the answer to this question can we choose whether or not to disbelieve it. Disbelieving is slow thinking.

Looking for information to refute something we already believe in goes against human nature. Instead, we are hard-wired to search for information that confirms our beliefs. Think about what evidence you would you gather if someone asked you these questions about the toothpaste you use: "Is this a good toothpaste? or is this a bad toothpaste?" Chances are that you'd gather evidence to prove that your toothpaste was a good toothpaste.

There is a little story about Socrates teaching the young Plato outside of Athens when a wayfarer crosses their way.

He asks Socrates, "Tell me, old man, how are the people of Athens? I heard that people here are quite unfriendly and treacherous."

"You are right," Socrates replied. "People you'll meet in Athens will be unfriendly and treacherous."

The stranger crossed his eyebrows, took a deep breath, and headed toward the city in a foul mood.

A few minutes later another wayfarer arrived to the town gates and asked Socrates, " Tell me, old man, how are the people of Athens? I heard that people here are very welcoming and amicable.

"You are right," said Socrates. "People you'll meet in Athens will be welcoming and amicable."

When the second visitor entered the city with a smile on his face, the young Plato couldn't contain his curiosity.

"Master, you told a lie to one of these people. You presented Athens in quite different ways."

"I didn't lie to either of them. What they believe, that they shall find."

The automatic acceptance of ideas, just because they confirm beliefs we currently hold, happens in fast thinking. Because we do it without question, it makes us susceptible to believing irrational and unlikely things. We often put more faith in our own intuition than is warranted. We are not an accurate judge of how much we should trust our own beliefs.

When do judgments reflect true expertise? In Kahneman's opinion, only when we have a stable environment with regular, predictable events we can observe and learn from. With prolonged time and practice, our intuitive skills become strengthened to the point where they can be trusted and considered to be a level of expertise.

Jumping to Conclusions

Since we know that fast thinking makes many errors, the best way to avoid these mistakes is to recognize situations when we are at risk of making snap decisions and take a breath long enough to engage our slow thinking. It is often when we need our slow thinking the most that we are least likely to use it.

Businesses and other groups are usually better than individuals in using slow thinking, thus avoiding frequent mistakes because, by their very nature, thinking and change within them takes longer time. They also have procedures in place that will help their decision makers to slow down and prevent hasty decisions.

When we are presented with difficult questions, we tend to try to answer an easier question instead. For example, when someone asks you what you think about something, you tend to answer the question how do you *feel* about it. This is not usually an intentional or conscious choice, but rather something our brains automatically do. Intuition and fast thinking kicks in, and we sometimes mistakenly jump at the first answer or solution that comes to mind, even when it doesn't sufficiently address the question or problem at hand.

Most of our thinking starts with fast thinking involving our feelings and initial impressions. Slow thinking gets involved when things are difficult to the point where they require a more deliberate process to solve them. Or when we are surprised and recognize a situation isn't normal in terms of what we expect to find in our current view of the world (held in our fast thinking) and requires further examination.

It would be exhausting to keep our mind at constant high alert and suspicion, questioning everything that comes in our way. Also, slow thinking consumes too much energy wasted on every single mundane decision we need to make. The best we can do is meet in the middle and recognize when we are in a situation where we could easily make mistakes and enlist the assistance of our slow thinking to help us avoid those mistakes.

When we don't have much information on a subject, we are at significant risk of jumping to conclusions. We know that fast thinking often enters autopilot mode and quickly springs to action. Kahneman refers to this tendency of jumping to conclusions with the following sentence, "What you see is all there is." Fast thinking focuses on the existing information and assumes that there is no other information out there to consider, or simply ignores if any information is missing. The snap judgments and impressions of fast thinking may get quickly adopted by our slow thinking and become an entrenched belief or bias that can lead to prejudice, incorrect judgments, and mistakenly trusting conspiracy theories.

Some common errors in reasoning people make when they rely on their fast thinking too much can include:

• Law of small numbers: trusting a small or unrepresentative sample of people expressing their opinions as being more reflective of the greater population than it really is, or accepting a limited amount of information or data as being enough to make a generalization about a larger group or trend.

• Illusion of understanding: we like stories that make sense and wrap things up in a neat and tidy bow. The illusion of understanding is cherry picking events that make sense to us and fit with the narrative we want to create in our minds while conveniently forgetting or dismissing the things that don't.

• Overconfidence: we overestimate the strength of our intuition and judgment by ignoring what we don't know and assuming that if nothing immediately comes to our mind that contradicts a belief or picture we already have, we must be correct. In a study in Daniel Kahneman's book, *Thinking, Fast and Slow*, Duke University asked the CFOs of large companies to make predictions about how they expected the S&P 500 to perform over the next year. The study found that there was no statistical connection between their predictions and its performance, but that didn't translate to the confidence level of the CFOs. Those who were the most overconfident in the study were also the most overconfident when it came to their own companies. As a result, they were willing to take greater business risks.

• Being overly optimistic: taking ill-advised risks because we assume that the odds will be in our favor and things will turn out better than the facts and data might suggest. We envision success rather than acknowledging the potential mistakes we might make. There is nothing inherently wrong with being optimistic and viewing the world through a positive lens as long as you stay realistic enough to keep it in check. The danger only lies in allowing our overconfidence in our abilities in the short term to cloud our decision making to the point where we take unnecessary risks without giving it careful thought and consideration.

• Loss aversion: Losses carry twice as much weight as gains. If you think over the gains and losses you have experienced in your life, you are probably more likely to remember more of the losses (when you use your fast thinking at least). Our fast thinking responds more to losses than gains. We don't like to lose, and we want to avoid it at all costs. This is called loss aversion.

How is it possible that we are overconfident and have loss aversion? Kahneman believes people either land on one end of the spectrum or the other with few people falling in between. He thinks people are either overconfident to the point where they ignore and dismiss risks as being unlikely and insignificant, or they are so afraid of losses that they try to avoid them completely by giving risk too much influence over their decisions and judgments.

To demonstrate loss aversion, Kahneman wrote about a study of professional golfers. The study examined their performance over 2.5 million putts to see if they were more focused on putting for par (avoiding a loss) or putting for birdie (gaining a stroke). The study found that the golfers were more focused and successful when they were putting to avoid losing a stroke.

It may seem hard to believe that they would be more concerned with putting not to lose than putting to win. If you have any doubts about that, consider the last time you were shooting hoops with your buddy or playing a game with family or friends. Who was more insistent that you should play another game? The one who won or the one who lost? Chances are it was the one who lost. Losing isn't fun and it sticks with us more than a win. No one wants to end at a low point.

As humans, it seems that we have an unlimited capacity to form feeling based opinions on almost any subject. We have a strong desire for the world to make sense, and we create stories and beliefs in our mind that help us meet that desire. We also are adept at underestimating our own ignorance. Often we don't even know what we don't know, and we seem largely content with that. We hold many of our beliefs because they are the beliefs of our loved ones or role models and the experts we look up to, not necessarily because they are based firmly on evidence.

At times, our intuition leads us astray, but there are also times when it can serve us well, so we would be wrong to dismiss it completely. The wise words once proclaimed by President Ronald Reagan, "trust but verify," might be the best approach we can take when it comes to our intuition.

Key Points:

• Our brains are hard wired to want to engage in fast thinking. Throughout history, the ability of humans to survive often depended on how quickly they could respond to a situation.

• Our brains can't rely on slow thinking for every decision we have to make. It consumes a great deal of energy that then becomes unavailable for us to use for other activities.

• The best solution is to be aware of when we are in situations where we are likely to make mistakes and engage our system 2, slow thinking, so we can avoid them.

- There are times when our intuition lets us down and guides us to illogical and incorrect conclusions. But it can still be a helpful tool for us. As critical thinkers, it is important that we "trust but verify" our intuition and objectively examine information to see if there is evidence to back it up or not.

Chapter 6: Staying clear of thinking errors

Data – Information- Knowledge – Understanding - Wisdom

What you know isn't nearly as important as *how* you know it.

There are two different types of thinking:

- Lower level, concrete thinking: This type of thinking is a more basic way of thinking. It involves making observations and gathering information and data. This is the base upon which the other type of thinking is built.

- Higher level, abstract thinking: This takes lower level thinking and raises it up a notch by digging deeper to find the connections between ideas and creating new thoughts and judgments that didn't previously exist.

It would be impossible to have this abstract thinking without the concrete thinking before it. Both types of thinking are important. We need to practice and strengthen our concrete thinking skills before we can advance to the higher level abstract thinking.[xlviii]

Much like the hierarchal levels of thinking identified in Bloom's taxonomy we discussed earlier, the relationship between data, information, knowledge, understanding, and wisdom also form a hierarchy.

- Data makes up the base of the pyramid. It is facts and figures. Data can be viewed in isolation and as being random.

- Information is the next step up in the hierarchy. Information includes the facts and figures of data that have been organized. The data begins to be grouped together.

- With knowledge, the data and information becomes more organized and it is examined for connections and links as it is no longer viewed in isolation.

- Understanding is the process by which someone can synthesize new knowledge from the previously held knowledge. It's the appreciation of the question "why?"

- Wisdom is evaluated understanding. It is built upon all the previous levels of consciousness, and specifically upon special subjects such as moral, ethical codes, and higher values. Wisdom aims to foster understanding about things that had previously not been understood, and thus goes beyond simple understanding. It creates new understanding. Wisdom asks difficult questions to which there is no simple answer, and in some cases, to which there can be no correct answer at all. These hard questions are often about judging between right and wrong, good and bad.[xlix]

Imagine the data-information-knowledge-understanding-wisdom hierarchy this way. Let's say you have books lying around your house. Those books are randomly scattered and looked at one at a time. This stage represents the data level of the pyramid. If you gather the books together and place them on a shelf, this would represent the information level, because you are beginning to view them as a group of books and organize them. If you look at the books and further organize them, putting them together by genre, topic, author, or series, you would be working at the knowledge level. If you knew what some of the similar books have in common and how they are connected, that would be understanding. If you could create new understanding, rethinking all the facts, details, knowledge, and understanding you have so far, and make an accurate value judgment of your personal library's information quality, that would be wisdom.

John Dewey, an American professor of education, looked at how people turn data into information in his Recipe for Education. In *The Philosopher* in 1934, he had some powerful insights that have an important message, which is relevant even today. He wrote:

> "The human mind does not learn in a vacuum; the facts presented for learning, to be grasped, must have some relation to the previous experience of the individual or to his present needs; learning proceeds from the concrete to the general, not from the general to the particular." [1]

When we can build on our prior experiences and make the data and information we are trying to learn connected and relevant to our lives, we will be much more successful in achieving deeper and higher levels of understanding. Dewey agreed that concrete lower level thinking must happen before higher level abstract thinking. He did not believe that information and knowledge could be viewed in isolation because in order for learning to take place, we have to explore connections.

> "Every individual is a little different from every other individual, not alone in his general capacity and character; the differences extend to rather minute abilities and characteristics, and no amount of discipline will eradicate them. The obvious conclusion of this is that uniform methods cannot possibly produce uniform results in education, that the more we wish to come to making everyone alike the more varied and individualized must the methods be."[li]

There is no such thing as a one size fits all method of teaching and learning. If we truly want to make sure that everyone can learn and achieve, we have to be willing to tailor our methods of teaching (or learning on our own) in such a way that the needs of the learner are being met and their strengths are built upon.

> "Individual effort is impossible without individual interest. There can be no such thing as a subject which in and by itself will furnish training for every mind. If work is not in itself interesting to the individual he cannot put his best efforts into it. However hard he may work at it, the effort does not go into the accomplishment of the work but is largely dissipated in a moral and emotional struggle to keep the attention where it is not held."[lii]

In order to be at our best in any learning or work endeavor, our heart has to be in it. If we try to force ourselves to learn something that doesn't capture our interest, we will spend a lot of our time and energy forcing ourselves to maintain focused on the task at hand and we will not be able to give it one hundred percent effort.

How to detect biases when we transform data into information?

How does data become information? Data is just facts. Information kicks in when we do something with those facts in order to organize or process those facts. Consider the following example.

Suppose I want to improve my overall physical health and lose some weight in the process. For a month, I record when and for how long I exercise and what I eat each day. These facts that I write down are the data I am collecting.

If I organize the data by making a chart and take it with me to my doctor's appointment to share the data with my doctor and talk to him about how despite exercising enough, I am not losing the weight I want, that data has turned into information because I have gone beyond just collecting it to organizing and processing it.

The transition from data to information isn't a crisp and clean one. We all carry our own biases with us throughout life, and when we begin to process and interpret data and turn it into information, we run the risk of making mistakes and allowing our biases to get in the way of our objectivity.

Let's look back at our example on weight loss. I had clearly collected data. I had written down the facts in my notebook of when I had exercised and for how long. Those facts aren't up for dispute as they are plain numbers. However, is it possible that I could or should have included more data? Like how strenuous my exercise regime was each day? When I recorded what I ate each day, would it have been more helpful to have a consistent way to measure the amount I ate as well?

I told my doctor that despite exercising enough, I wasn't achieving the weight loss goal I wanted. Was that a fact or my opinion? What did I base it on? Was it based on my doctor's recommendation? Research I had read? One expert's opinion? Social media forums? My own preconceived notion? It is definitely an opinion because so many value judgments went into my seemingly simple little statement. There were plenty of opportunities for my personal biases to creep in and affect my judgment.

Strong critical thinkers recognize that there is no way to completely escape our biases. The best we can hope for is that by increasing our awareness of them, we can keep them in check by questioning and challenging them. That is how we strengthen our critical thinking and decision making skills.

Asking questions is crucial. Consider the following questions presented by Daniel Kahneman:

- What might be the biases of the people presenting an idea or recommendation? Some of the most common are they might be overconfident, have a strong connection to past experiences, or be most concerned with their own self-interest and well-being.

- Do those making a recommendation really feel passionately about what they recommend? Chances are high they do, otherwise they wouldn't recommend it.

- Did people reach a conclusion just because that's what the others in the group decided and they wanted to fit in and go along with the group? Or were dissenting opinions also discussed and considered?

Dr. Kahneman believes it is important to not leave the decision making process completely up to chance. He recommends assembling a team of people who are willing and skilled at challenging the group's consensus and encouraging everyone to weigh and consider all viewpoints, even opposing ones.

De-biasing

Since we know we can't completely eliminate our biases, we need to try to limit the detrimental impacts they can have on the objectivity and rationality of our decisions and judgments.

It is important that we are aware when one of our cognitive biases is activated and make a conscious choice to overcome that bias. We need to be aware of the impact the bias has on our decision making process and our life. Then we can choose an appropriate de-biasing strategy to combat it. After we have implemented a strategy, we should check in again to see if it worked in the way we had hoped. If it did, we can move on and make an objective and informed decision. If it didn't, we can try the same strategy again or implement a new one until we are ready to make a rational judgment.

Luckily, we have metacognitive strategies at our disposal. Metacognition is when we are conscious and aware of the thought processes that lead us to make decisions and form judgments. It allows us to understand the mistakes in reasoning we might make as we process information. Metacognition enables us to recognize our own biases as well as the biases of others and to select strategies that will help us to address and overcome those biases.

There are some general de-biasing strategies that can help to mitigate almost any bias and reduce its negative impact:

- Changing the way we present information to others by making it more relatable, relevant, and easily understood will make others more likely to judge our information on its merits instead of just tuning it out or having a strong emotional reaction to it.

- Keeping things simple and to the point. Making information easier for others to process and remember.

- Having steps in place for how you want to address new information you are presented with will make you slow down your thought process and be more reflective instead of rushing to judgment.

Sometimes a more specific de-biasing strategy is more helpful in overcoming a cognitive bias. Some examples are:

- Reducing your reliance on subjective memory.

  Our emotions can distort the reality of past events. Rosy retrospection bias causes people to remember events from the past more positively than they actually happened. A helpful way to overcome this bias is to write down an objective record that you can refer to later to accurately refresh your memory. For example, if you end a relationship because it is unhealthy, but you suspect you may be tempted to take your ex back in the future, it may help to write down exactly why you felt the need to end the relationship so you can remind yourself later if need be.

- Considering alternative outcomes to past events.

  Another way our minds can distort the reality of past events is through choice-supportive bias, which causes people to focus on the positives while ignoring the negative consequences of a choice they made after the fact. For example, if you bought a new car, you might focus on the reasonable price you paid, the great interior features of the car, and the nice exterior appearance while ignoring the costs you spent on repairs or the low miles per gallon it gets when you drive. A good way to overcome this bias is to come up with a small list of alternative choices you could have made (in this case other cars you might have purchased).

- Creating psychological distance.

  Often people fall prey to the spotlight effect in which they overestimate how much attention others pay to them and judge them negatively for making mistakes. We are so used to viewing the world only from our own perspective that we tend to project our feelings and judgments about ourselves onto others and assume that they are judging us harshly when in reality they are too concerned with their own problems to even notice our actions let alone pass judgment on us. We can help to overcome this bias if we try to see ourselves from the viewpoint of others.[liii]

Key Points

- There are two types of thinking: lower level concrete thinking in which we tend to view things more in isolation and higher level abstract thinking in which we understand the connections between them. Both types of thinking are important, and we have to strengthen and develop our concrete thinking skills before we can develop our abstract thinking skills.

- Data, information, and knowledge are related. Data is basic facts and figures that are often viewed as random and in isolation. Information occurs when we organize the data and begin to process it. Knowledge occurs when we further organize the data and information and see the connections that exist between ideas.

- If we can make information relevant and connected to a learner's past experiences, greater and deeper learning will take place.

- There is no one size fits all method when it comes to teaching and learning. We have to take into account the individual learner's strengths, needs, and interests in order to help them achieve their full potential.

- Transitioning from data to information can result in errors in reasoning and biases clouding our judgment.

- We can't eliminate our biases completely, but we can mitigate them and reduce their impact if we are aware of our biases and make a conscious choice to implement strategies to help us question and challenge them so we can keep them in check.

Chapter 7: Critical Reading and Writing

Critical Reading

Critical readers are critical thinkers with a book. They know reading is about so much more than learning facts. It is when we really dig deeper and think about what we read that we gain knowledge and can claim ownership over that learning.

Critical readers refuse to accept what they read at face value simply because it is in print. They read actively, questioning and challenging ideas as they go. Much like a judge, they are constantly considering the strengths and weaknesses of the argument the author is trying to present.

Just as we have to make a conscious choice to develop, practice, and strengthen our critical thinking skills, we should also do the same with our critical reading skills. The problem is these skills aren't always stressed in our schools.

Teachers and schools are under a lot of pressure to get their students to perform well on high stakes tests. These tests determine what teachers teach. Teachers present only the information they have time for and think is most beneficial for students to learn. Students receive higher test scores when they can recall what they were taught.

This means that teachers instruct their students how to summarize information rather than to select it. Schools want students who respect authority and experts so, challenging and questioning the information teachers present is discouraged rather than practiced and encouraged.

This isn't exactly the perfect recipe for developing critical reading skills. But that doesn't make critical reading any less essential. Just because the importance of this skill isn't currently taught, doesn't mean that it isn't imperative later in life. People who aren't strong critical readers can really struggle in their profession.

Just because some information appears in print doesn't mean it's true. While we would like to think every author has voraciously researched their topic and educated him or herself in the best and most current knowledge available, this is not always the case. Like all people, it is possible for authors to have gathered weak evidence and drawn incorrect conclusions. Authors can be wrong, misinformed, confused, or even dishonest. The data and information used to support arguments can be out of date. It is important to read with a critical mind and have a healthy dose of skepticism.

How to make sure that what you read is up-to-date, relevant, and truthful?

Make certain what you are reading is from a reputable source. Make sure the academic journal or other publisher is known for being thorough and using universally accepted methods of research. There are fields of science that contain many opposing expert opinion. Therefore even an academic proofreading doesn't guarantee there are no smaller or bigger mistakes or biases in the "scientific work."

Be aware of the biases and interests the author or publisher may have in presenting the data in a certain way. Look for the author to communicate his or her argument early in the writing and to provide clear and consistent support for it throughout. This makes readers believe the author is trying to be honest, and it gives readers an opportunity to judge arguments from beginning to end.

Higher level thinking and knowledge comes when we are able to move beyond just accumulating data to organizing those thoughts and ideas and digging deeper to uncover connections between them. There are a few quick and easy ways that critical readers can check the organization, methodology, and detail foci of an author.

First, check the topic of the book? Is it a relevant, important topic or rather a trendy one more likely to sell? Books released by big publishing companies are aimed to sell – the publishing house wants to make money. They try to widen the scientific and social circles of the book topic to attract a larger audience – buyers. Critical readers consider why an author wrote a book when evaluating the voracity of its arguments. Was it just to make a lot of money? Was it to document the importance of an event? Was it to earn the author credibility in academic circles? Was it to provide reputable research or to advance their personal religious, social, scientific, or political viewpoint?

Critical readers evaluate the sources and research methodology used by the author to make sure they are credible. They examine whether the author presents their opinions as facts without specific evidence to back them up and whether or not they are willing to present and dispute arguments and viewpoints that differ from their own.

In order to check an author's methodology, the guiding framework they used to write their book that impacts the lens through which they view the subject and determine which information is important and relevant enough to be included in their writing, consider the following:

- Theoretical vs. Empirical:
   Is the author more reliant on ideas and theories or observations and measureable data

to prove his point? This may not be easy to figure out as most authors attempt to use both. Examine the text carefully to see which one the author utilizes the most, as it will give you some insight on the type of support they value most in drawing their conclusions.

- Nomothetic vs. Idiographic:
  Nomothetic evidence in writing and research looks to take specific data or information gathered and generalizes it to a larger group (moves from the part to the whole). Idiographic evidence takes a generalization of a large group and brings it down to an individual example (moves from the whole to the part). Critical readers need to be sure that the author didn't take any illogical leaps in order to make generalizations and connections to the larger group.[liv]

- Cause vs. Correlation:

  These two words get mixed up in people's minds so often that you might assume they are interchangeable, but this is simply not the case. Causation means that one event causes another. Correlation means that there seems to be a relationship between two things that is greater than would be possible by random chance, but one event does not necessarily cause the other – there are other possibilities that could result in the same outcome. All too often authors jump to the conclusion that one thing is caused by another without sufficient proof. We must always be aware of the natural bias that tends to want to find causation, even when it may not exist as it can often lead to incorrect conclusions.

- Statistical Answers vs. Ideological Hypothesis
  Statistics can be made to show almost anything. It all depends on the lens through

which we view them. We have a tendency to give emphasis to the statistics that prove our point while we ignore or dismiss the ones that don't. Authors, researchers, businesses, politicians, and others can manipulate what the statistics actually reveal by only telling us the part of the story they like and omitting the rest. Or they can make simple mistakes in the way they work with or interpret the data that make them overly confident in their findings and their importance. Critical readers should be on guard against being satisfied with only a partial picture.

Take some time to look into an author's credentials. They want to know what it is in the author's background, education, and experience that make her an expert or authority on the subject about which she has written. Look for the types of biases the author may bring to the table that may have influenced her writing. Everyone has biases so try to assess whether the author's bias may have clouded her ability to objectively form and present her arguments based on evidence.

In addition to considering the author's motivation for writing a book, critical readers recognize they should also assess their own motivation for selecting a certain book or article to read. Was it because it was recommended reading in academic circles, reinforced views they already held, was identified as an important contribution on a specific topic, presented a minority viewpoint, or it just caught their eye at the bookstore? If it is something they just stumbled across, it may not be representative of the consensus thoughts on the topic or be written by an author with expertise and authority on the subject matter.

If it is a book recommended to them by another person, they are depending upon the judgment of that person to tell them it is a worthy source of information. Critical readers recognize a book or article they have chosen to read is only one piece of the puzzle in their quest for the truth. They are fully aware there are many more out there that should be explored on the path toward deeper knowledge as lifelong learners.

Another consideration of critical readers as they evaluate text is when the text was written. Why is that so important? While some facts and information are timeless, most are not. Facts and data keep changing over time. We constantly make new discoveries that warrant the modification or abandonment of previously believed ideas. It is imperative that we are always open to questioning and challenging ideas and beliefs to make sure they can withstand the test of time and aren't outdated and obsolete. Paying attention to when text is written also provides a critical reader with some very important context as to what may be impacting and guiding the assumptions that are being made. If a book or article is written in a different time, its content could be quite different based on the current events occurring simultaneously.

How to remember what you read?
Some books have so much value and wisdom. But what good would is it to read that wisdom if you can't remember what you've read? Immerse yourself in the text and interact with it. It is an investment of time and energy that will pay off in long-term knowledge you can gain.
Research has showed that we typically forget ninety-eight percent of what we read even when we read carefully. So if we're only going to remember two percent, we should focus on finding the two percent that matters.

Critical readers want to preserve that knowledge. It is a lot like why we put our money in the bank. We want it to be safe and waiting for us when we want to use it. That's the approach that critical thinkers take when it comes to recording their new knowledge, so it will be available to them when they need it.

There are two ways they go about taking what they read and increasing the likelihood that they will remember it and be able to access it when they want to: note-taking and summaries. When critical readers take notes or write summaries, they are not trying to simply regurgitate the author's words. They are actively engaged with the text and are digging deeper to try to find the insights and knowledge that are most relevant and important to them.

When you actively think about what you read and write down the key points in your own words, you are making your own connections and uncovering your own feelings and thoughts on a topic that you may never have known you had before. Not to mention that you will be much more likely to remember what you read because you are making it your own. Here are some suggestions on how to take effective notes to summarize text:

- Don't interrupt your reading to take notes. Read the selection in its entirety until you reach a natural break point. Then take a moment to reflect on what you've read.

- Identify the parts of the text that resonate the most with you as being important and relevant.

- Write those VIPs (very important points) down in your own words. This makes your learning your own.

- If there is a large portion of the text that you feel should be included in your notes, don't try to write it all down unless you won't be able to access the text later. Instead write a one-sentence summary of what that section is about, and then write down where it can be found in the book or text for future reference.

- Organize your notes in the way that makes sense to you. They do not need to be in the same order they appeared in the text.

Critical Writing

Critical writing is when an author refuses to accept the conclusions of others without evaluating their arguments and evidence. It is the careful consideration of all sides of an argument and evidence to reach objective, informed, rational conclusions. Strong critical writers recognize and acknowledge that there are limitations in everyone's evidence, arguments, and conclusions, but they do their level best to present the most supported, well thought out case they can.

Strong critical writers make sure they support any claims they make with evidence. They know that anything they say that is not universally accepted or is controversial needs to have even more evidence to back it up if it is going to persuade the reader.

Critical writers do not only concentrate on giving reasons why readers should believe their conclusions, but they also present opposing arguments and cite evidence that will refute and discredit them. This serves to further strengthen the author's position in the minds of readers.

It is not necessary for a critical writer to come up with every new idea completely on their own. It is perfectly acceptable for them to examine other ideas or opinions and add their own thoughts and evaluations of it.

How to prepare for a critical writing?

Critical writers take the time to prepare before they begin writing. They do their homework by doing research. They know their topic well. They read a wide variety of sources on the topic and take notes on the insights that stand out to them the most as being relevant and important. They learn from others who have experience writing on the subject. Strong critical writers are willing to invest a lot of time and energy before they even write the first word because they understand that preparation will pay off in the long run when they are able to present stronger more effective arguments.

Critical writing focuses on giving evidence and arguments to support the author's conclusions and disprove or dispute other positions that stand in disagreement. There will be some claims that are already largely accepted or seem like common sense that writers can assume their readers will pretty readily accept. But if they present new or controversial conclusions that may require a leap or shift in thinking, critical writers are aware that they must provide sufficient solid support in order to persuade others to their line of thought. They don't shy away from opposing viewpoints. They share them and face them head on by offering evidence to dispute them.

Using references is a helpful tool to support ideas with evidence. Citing references in a work encourages readers to believe the author is honest and isn't trying to take credit for ideas that were not their own. Reference gives readers additional sources to access more information on the topic, examine arguments made by others, and check where the author is drawing his conclusions.

References can also remind writers where their guiding ideas came from and act as a check to make sure their thoughts and ideas aren't incorrect and obsolete.

Skilled critical writers keep their audience in mind when they choose what to include in their text. They should be laser focused on the topic and relevant information connected to that. They need to put themselves in the readers' shoes and direct their writing toward the questions the readers would want answered rather than their own personal interest on the topic.

They need to be cognizant of whether they can reasonably expect readers to have a shared base of common knowledge or opinions from which to build upon. If an author's readers are diverse and come from various geographic areas, socioeconomic levels, generations, or cultures, they may not be able to count on this and some additional background knowledge or references may need to be provided.

If readers have to struggle to remember one onerous point at the same time that you are trying to process the next challenging point, a lot of the message and flow of your text will be lost.

Keep your sentences short, simple, and to the point. If highly technical terms are necessary, explain them in layman's terms as much as possible. Otherwise, select a language that is not too technical or difficult for your audience to understand.

Just answering the guiding question of your work isn't enough. A guiding question is the "where are we going" question. It acts as a lighthouse – a beacon of light on which to fix your eyes to be sure you don't veer off course. Everything an author writes should be in an attempt to answer the guiding question. They must make it clear to the readers that they have answered it completely and definitively. They recognize that it's imperative they clearly demonstrate that they arrived at their conclusion from the evidence they presented and that it answers the guiding question laid out in the book or article.

All critical writing should have the following components:

• A guiding question to tell the reader what the author will be writing about.

- An outline to act as a road map of how the author will answer the guiding question.
- A sense of flow and connection between paragraphs and chapters easily and logically moving the reader from one idea to the next.
- A valid conclusion based on evidence (this is the "we're here" portion of the text).

Every word that a critical writer chooses communicates a message; the words and information they use as well as the ones they do not are deliberate choices. Everything has a meaning down to how the facts and arguments are arranged in the writing.

Keywords communicate to the reader where the author's focus lies. They show readers how the argument is laid out to help and guide them through, the reading pointing out what the author believes is most important and where the argument is going next.

Authors who want to present another argument that supports their viewpoint might use keywords such as: similarly, another, or likewise. If the goal is to point out a difference between arguments or viewpoints, the author might select: however, on the other hand, conversely, or but as their key words. Authors who are trying to dispute a criticism of their argument might use the keywords: but, even so, still, or nonetheless.

Transitions are used by writers to keep the flow of their work. They act as links connecting ideas smoothly one after the other. Transitions introduce new ideas (such as first of all or recent studies show), begin new paragraphs (such as next or finally), signal that a statement is further proof of something already shared (for example, further, similarly or likewise), or point out a different viewpoint (such as on the other hand, conversely, or nonetheless). [lv]

Critical writers may also use intermediate conclusions. An intermediate conclusion is any conclusion that the author makes which isn't the final conclusion. A statement supported by evidence that the author uses to back up their main conclusion. In essence it is a smaller argument within the main argument.

Let's consider this example. Japan has one of the lowest birth rates in the world averaging just over seven births per 1,000 people. Currently the retirement age in Japan is sixty-two years old with the average life expectancy being nearly eighty-four years of age. By 2060, the Japanese government estimates that sixty percent of the country's population will be over sixty-five years old.[lvi]

If I am making an argument with the main conclusion that in order to support an aging population Japan will either have to raise its retirement age or the younger workers will have to increase their productivity in the workplace, I might make other intermediate conclusions along the way that support my main conclusion. An example of an intermediate conclusion might be due to a low birth rate, even though Japan's population is living longer, its overall population will begin to decline in number which will result in fewer people in the workforce.

Critical writers are skilled at getting their message across in a way that is informative, effective, persuasive, interesting, and easily understood by their audience. It is a craft like critical thinking and critical reading that requires extra effort and practice to strengthen and develop.

Key Points:
- Being a critical reader and writer require a skill set that can prove invaluable to people in many areas of their personal and professional lives.

- Critical readers refuse to believe something simply because it appears in print. They are actively engaged as they read challenging materials and questioning the author's conclusions and assumptions as they go.

- Critical readers are keenly aware of the biases that both readers and writers bring to the table and are on guard against them. They evaluate an author's credentials to see what enables them to write with authority on a topic. They make sure they get their evidence and information from reputable sources. They pay attention to when books or articles are written to make sure the information in them is not outdated or obsolete.

- Critical writers are the careful thoughtful organizers of a debate in print. They present not only their own viewpoints and assumptions, but opposing ones as well. They state their conclusion clearly and lay out the evidence they have accumulated that supports it in an attempt to persuade their readers to agree with their line of thinking. They are confident in their positions and do not shy away from differing points of view because they believe they have evidence firmly on their side.

- Critical writers have the added challenge of presenting their arguments in language that can be clearly followed by their audience. They must present informed and convincing arguments in a way that is interesting and well received by their readers. It takes time and practice to strengthen and develop those skills.

Chapter 8: Empower Your Logic Toolkit

When you hear the word logic, what type of person do you associate it with? My bet is that you visualize some old math professor or nerdy scientist who is slouching over a thousand plus page textbook. Some people like that, indeed, have excellent logical skills, but that's rather a mere coincidence. Logic and science don't always walk hand in hand.

What is the aim of science? It is to draw universal, general conclusions from a limited amount of samples. While scientific research and conclusions are the motors that take our civilization forward, strictly speaking, scientific methods are illogical. By the definition of logicians, the inductive reasoning of science is not logical. They prefer deductive reasoning, that's what they accept as logical.

Inductive arguments are based on the estimation that something is likely or probable. Inductive reasoning is when we take a limited amount of evidence and generalize it to draw a conclusion. There is a danger in inductive reasoning that the next piece of evidence we discover might completely disprove the argument.

Deductive arguments don't leave room for probability. If the premises are true, then the conclusion has to be. The conclusion flows directly from the premises. Deductive reasoning conclusions tend to be much more solid and lasting. They are more likely to withstand the test of time and new evidence that may come up.

Deductive reasoning is more certain, but also less likely to uncover things we didn't already know. The issue with deductive reasoning is that it can't bring new information to the table as it only works with existing ones.

In real life situations, many arguments are inductive thus, at the end of the day, illogical.
In this section I will talk about how to use the type of logic –called informal logic - that can help people to have better arguments, and improved deductive reasoning.

Informal logic is everyday logic. It involves evaluating real-life arguments in ordinary layman's language. This logic is the kind you are most likely to encounter in the informal arguments found in your daily life. It is when you argue with your spouse about whose turn it is to take out the trash, when you argue with family members over dinner about the political issues of the day, or have a heated debate over what type of music should play on the radio in the car. Informal logic deals with real-life disagreements between two parties who are firmly convinced that their opinion is correct.

If you wonder what other type of logic is there, well formal logic, of course. Formal logic uses symbols and special language to deal with arguments. When each of the argument points are reduced to some kind of symbol, the logician can have a more transparent view on the situation and manipulate the symbols to make sense of the situation just as a chemist creates complex chemical compounds. Using this type of logic on everyday situations is tedious, slow, and frankly, unnecessary. Just think of it as your hairdo – you don't make a strict, well-shaped hair just to wash the dishes.

When we are engaged in our daily life we rarely point out our assumptions to others. We think the assumptions are understood by them so we head straight for our conclusion. In these disagreements we tend to start with our position and then go back to fill in the reasons why we believe it is true.

In philosophy arguments are presented as two or more statements which can be true or false. The statements, also called as premises, lead to a conclusion. If the argument is sound, then as long as the premises are true, the conclusion will also be true. Imagine the following argument your wife tells you. She says:
- You're a lazy husband! You always sleep in late! Only lazy people wake up so late!

In the language of critical thinking we would group the argument of your wife like this:

- Premise #1: Lazy people sleep in late.
- Premise #2: You sleep in late.
- Conclusion: You are a lazy person.

Is the conclusion valid based on the premises? This is not a sound (valid) argument because lazy people aren't the only ones who sleep in late. Some people work different shifts which affect when they sleep and it has nothing to do with them being lazy. Some people are sick so they sleep in late. There are many reasons a person might sleep in late. However, trying to point our this error in reasoning to an angry wife is a hardly going to change her opinion, which leads to the conclusion that by giving a logical structure to real-life problems seldom solves the problem itself.

A sound or valid argument is one if the premises are true then the conclusion is definitely true too. This error in reasoning in the example means that there is a problem with the structure of the argument. When it comes to real-life arguments and informal logic, we may not be overly concerned about the structure of the argument, but by examining the premises that lead to the conclusions a little more closely, we may uncover the real concerns in the disagreement.

Another example of a real-life argument is a very timely one in the United States. With frequent mass shootings sadly taking place in the country, an impassioned debate can often be heard on both sides of the argument over gun control. Here is one argument that those in favor of gun control sometimes make:

- Premise #1: Owning guns leads people to commit violence and mass shootings to other people.

- Premise #2: Something that leads people to commit violence and injure or kill others in mass shootings is bad.

- Conclusion: Therefore, owning guns is bad.

Let's traduce this example to the language of formal logic. In formal logic, only premises and conclusions can be true or false. Arguments are considered valid or invalid. Formal logic offers an objective way to check the structure of an argument to be sure it is logical and sound. Arguments presented through formal logic would look like this:

- If A then B.
- If B then C.
- Therefore, if A then C.

Let's rewrite our gun control example to formal logic:

- If A then B: Gun ownership leads to awful things.
- If B then C: *If* something is awful, it should be banned.
- Therefore, if A then C: Therefore, gun ownership should be banned.

Premises don't have to be true or proven, but the conclusion is only expected to be true *if* the premises are.

There is more to determining if this informal argument is a valid one. We need to examine not only what the argument says, but also what it doesn't say. While some people may believe that it is wrong to own guns in any situation, far more people realize that gun ownership alone does not *always* lead people to commit violence and mass shootings on others. Many people own guns without incident. A small percentage of gun owners are violent with other people and participate in mass shootings. The terrible tragic events occur more often than not when people have mental health issues or a history of criminal or violent behavior in their past. This renders the argument as invalid.

Based on the reasoning above, the formal logic structure should rather look like this:
- Premise #1: If A then sometimes B.
- Premise #2: If B then C.
- Conclusion: Therefore, if A then C.

In other words:
- Gun ownership sometimes leads to awful things.

- If something is awful, it should be banned.
- Guns should be banned.

However, this argument is more invalid than the previous one because if the A is not necessarily B, the it doesn't matter what C we bring in the picture, for sure, the argument won't be valid.

Just because this kind of argumentative reasoning is invalid, it doesn't mean that the right decision in the case of guns is to allow anyone to have them with little or no control. The solution of the gun problem requires much more than logical reasoning, unfortunately. We don't try to make sense of our country's greatest break lines, just interpreting the structure of arguments through formal and informal logic.

Unnecessary and Insufficient

Another method to add into our logic toolkit is assessing formal and informal logic and the structure of arguments is in terms of insufficient and unnecessary conditions. Some decisions have to meet the necessary conditions in order to consider them logical. Let's consider the following example:

Newborns need feeding to survive. If newborns go without feeding for several days, they will eventually die. Nutrients like breast milk are a necessary condition for the baby's survival. Ultimately, no human will survive without food.

I would like for all babies in the world to be healthy and content as they grow up. This means that giving them food alone isn't sufficient to make babies healthy and happy. We know that food is necessary for their survival, but so are water, air, and shelter. Babies would be unhealthy and unable to live long without any of them.

That makes food a *necessary but insufficient* condition for a baby's survival.

Let's take this reasoning a step further. I said I want babies to be healthy and content, so what if I introduce a comfortable bed into their room? While it would probably add to their comfort level, so could many other things like a fun toy, a warm bath, a mother's touch, or unconditional attention.

That makes the fancy bed an *unnecessary condition* because babies can be healthy and content even in a regular bed. It is also an insufficient condition because the bed is not enough to keep the babies healthy, as they still require food, water, air, and shelter in order to survive.

What are the necessary conditions to a baby's survival? Think about them for a moment. It is not a difficult task and probably within three minutes you could come up with a page-long of things. I bet you didn't think about keeping rats out of the baby's room to keep the baby safe. (Have you seem the Disney cartoon The Lady and The Tramp? It has a crazy scene at the end where a rat is about to attack a baby.) You see, just because you didn't add the rat example to your list, you didn't exhaust all the necessary conditions to a baby's survival.

The bottom line of this brainstorming is that in real life situations, trying to bring the necessary and sufficient conditions to the table are often impractical, and thinking of every single condition is almost impossible. Thus this exercise better serves only to train your logic muscle, trying to identify and categorize which conditions are necessary but insufficient, which are unnecessary and so on.

What are hidden assumptions?

Hidden assumptions are something we all bring to the table. When we are acting in our capacity as critical thinkers and readers, we need to examine the arguments that others make through their eyes. As we attempt to better understand and dig deeper into their point of view, we will be more equipped to find the hidden assumptions they make so that we can question and challenge them if they are biased or invalid.

It is not only the hidden assumptions of others we should examine, but our own as well. When we frequently challenge and question our own beliefs to be sure they are relevant and supported by evidence, we can find problems and gaps in our viewpoint we may need to strengthen to improve our own arguments and conclusions.

The lens through which we view the world can be shaped by a variety of factors that we may not even consciously be aware of including:

- race, culture, and ethnicity,
- educational background,
- age and family status (single, married, parent, person with many siblings, etc.),
- socioeconomic status,
- sex and gender,

- religious beliefs (or absence thereof),
- opinions of our peers and others we like and respect.

Finding our own hidden assumptions or those of others can be helpful to us as they enable us to stay a step ahead. We can better predict the arguments that might be presented and how differ from or attempt to dispute ours. Then we can be proactive and conduct additional research to try to strengthen our assumptions to be better prepared to address challenges that may arise.

The Laws of Thought by Aristotle

Aristotle, an Ancient Greek philosopher and scientist who is still widely regarded today as one of the greatest thinkers in history for his significant and lasting contributions to almost every area of human knowledge, had a deep interest in logic, which led him to develop his laws of thought.

He believed that they are necessary conditions for human thought to occur:

- *Law of identity:* "Whatever is, is." This means that everything that exists has its own specific identity formed by the sum of all of its individual characteristics. It can only have its own identity and it can't exist as anything else.

- *Law of non-contradiction*: "Nothing can both be and not be." This means that nothing can exist and not exist at the same time. No statement can be both true and false.

We know that even Aristotle shouldn't have his ideas accepted at face value without being questioned and challenged. While the laws of thought are one of Aristotle's peak "brain children," he also had a fair share of inaccurate or foolish opinions: like when he said that women were incapable of thinking logically and were more like pets than full-value, thinking human beings. His mentor, Plato, shared quite the opposite opinion, considering women also great thinkers.

This story brings us to another controversial, but general question, namely are males more suited for logical thinking than females? While traditional opinions would seem to support the belief of males being better at logic, there is actually no evidence to back it up. No matter the thinking task, there is very little difference in the ways that men and women think. Research has measured the differences in written thinking, intuitive thinking, thinking in analogies, etc. Even when slight differences in their thinking are detected, it's nothing a little education can't fix to level the playing field.

The place where the most significant difference has been identified is in formal logic and math. As we discussed earlier, formal logic is expressed in symbols instead of words, which seems to play to the strengths of males more than females. This may be because the information is presented in a more abstract way and more easily manipulated.

Expectations and preconceived notions can have a measurable impact on performance. In 1999, Canadian psychologist, Steven Spencer, conducted an experiment in which he gave two groups of students the same test of logical reasoning. The only difference between the tests was that one group was told the goal of the test was to assess the gap between the ways males and females think logically while the other group did not receive any priming. The girls in the group that was told there was a gap between the logic of boys and girls performed worse on the task than the girls in the group that wasn't led to believe there was a logic gap between genders. The stereotypes people hold run the risk of becoming a self-fulfilling prophecy, and we must be on guard against that.

The conclusion of this section is that informal logic does not seem to give males the same advantage over females. Informal logic is where critical thinking skills reside. So ladies, don't let anything discourage you!

What makes an argument convincing?

Affirming the antecedent

True premises don't automatically lead to true conclusions – a valid argument that is structured well is needed to lead us there. While critical thinkers tend to focus more on informal logic than formal logic, there are benefits we can gain from looking at our arguments in the form of letters and symbols. The easiest way to form a convincing argument is to set it up and structure it as a hypothetical syllogism, an "if-then" statement that claims if one thing happens, then another thing will happen, and then taking it one step further to prove that the first thing is really true. This is an argument called *affirming the antecedent* (or modus ponens in Latin).

It is important to check the structure of the argument to be sure it is logical, and often the simplest way to do this is to look at it in letters and symbols. It is possible to start off with an untrue premise and still end up with a valid argument, but it makes the job a lot more difficult because untrue assumptions make for unsound arguments, which are a lot harder to convince people to believe.

The correct structure of an argument shown in symbols would be:

- If A, then B.
- A.
- Therefore B.

An example might be:

- *If* students study for a test *then* they will perform better.
- The students studied for a test.
- Therefore they must have performed better on the test.

This argument is by no means definitive and universally accepted. There can be disagreements over the premise questioning what it means for students to study for a test. What amount of time is needed to study? Are there specific skills or strategies that need to be utilized in order to constitute studying? Is there a certain environment or conditions necessary for studying to take place? Since there is some ambiguity about whether the starting assumption is true, there is uncertainty about the conclusion that is drawn.

Here is a valid argument to affirm the antecedent:
- If you touch the hot stove, you'll get burned.
- You touched the hot stove.
- Therefore, you got burned.

This argument is valid because the conclusion simply reinforces what the hypothetical premise implied. The truth of A would be sufficient for the truth of B. If we accept A to be true, we may conclude that B is true as well.[lvii]

Denying the consequent

Another valid way to make an argument is to *deny the consequent (*or modus tollens in Latin). Instead of proving the beginning part of the statement (A) is true, this structure focuses on proving the ending part of the statement (B) false. It assumes that if the consequent (what happens after) is false, then the antecedent (what happens before) is also false.

The structure of this type of argument written in symbols would look like:

- If A, then B.
- Not B.
- Therefore not A.

An example might be:

- *If* children have too much screen time each day, then they will be obese.
- My children are not obese.
- Therefore my children do not have too much screen time each day.

While the argument is structurally organized to be valid, it is ultimately still unsound because there are other factors that could be in play such as a child's genetic makeup, metabolism, diet, and the amount of physical activity they participate in. This can allow others to question the conclusion that was drawn.

Consider this hypothetical syllogism for denying the consequent:
- If God wanted us to fly, he would have given us wings.
- He didn't give us wings.
- Therefore he didn't want us to fly.

In this example we denied the consequent (B), which helped us deny the antecedent (A), too.[lviii]

Recognizing fallacies

Fallacies are invalid arguments. They can be caused by a problem in the way the argument was built. Even true premises can lead to a false conclusion. We want to detect and avoid these errors in reasoning because they can mislead and misinform us. How can we recognize fallacies before they lead us astray?

Imagine that you are having an argument with a friend about whether or not dolphins breathe with gills. You know that dolphins live in the water and need oxygen to survive. You know that fish live in the water, breathe with gills, and need oxygen to survive. We will assume for the sake of this argument that you are unsure about whether or not dolphins breathe with gills. Here is how looking at the argument through the lens of structure and logic can be helpful in recognizing a fallacy.

- Overarching premise: All fish live in water and have gills.
- Secondary premise: All dolphins live in water.
- Conclusion: All dolphins have gills.

The two premises are true, but they are incomplete which results in them leading to a false conclusion.

There are several species of animals that live in the water that do not breathe with gills like fish do. Starfish, whales, sea turtles, seals, and sea lions are a few of these. Dolphins swim to the surface of the water to inhale oxygen through their blowhole on top of their head and they breathe with lungs. They do not have gills. Dolphins are mammals, not fish, and all mammals have lungs.

Using syllogisms and applying formal and informal logic to everyday events is a very good training practice for the critical thinker's brain. However, don't fall into the rabbit hole where you try to detect fallacies everywhere and analyze the world through premise 1-2 and conclusion structure. Remember that most of everyday thinking relies on inductive reasoning, thus it draws conclusions from only limited evidence. We use them, even though by logical definition they are invalid and can be easily contested.

Why do we use them anyway then? Because the alternative thinking method is deductive reasoning, which has solid and valid arguments like 2+2=4, humans are mortal and such. The problem with deductive reasoning is that whatever is a one hundred percent valid argument is something we already knew. That's why it's valid, because it uses already proven facts.

What logic to use then? Think of logic as a guide that aids to make more reasoned arguments rather than something very abstract. Whenever you make an argument, follow these steps:
- Make sure you're not contradicting yourself.
- If you are writing, make sure to state your main viewpoint early.
- When you are presenting an opposing viewpoint, use words that indicate it like "on the contrary" or "conversely."

- Explain how the contradictory opinions of your viewpoints can be resolved, leaving your opinion the valid one.
- If there is no solution to the contradictory opinions of your views, make that clear.

Logic Exercises

Now it's time to put our logic to the test! Try to solve these five logic exercises created by teach-nology.com, and then check the answers to find out how you did.[lix]

1. **Ship-Wrecked**

A train leaves New York City and travels toward Los Angeles at 100 mph. Three hours later; a second train leaves Los Angeles and travels toward New York City at 200 MPH. If it is exactly 2000 miles between the two cities, which train will be closer to New York City when they meet?

2. **The Camels**

A father told his two sons to ride their camels to a faraway city to determine who would inherit his fortune. The one whose camel was the slowest would receive the inheritance. The brothers, after going as slowly as possible for days, asked a wise old man for his advice. Once they heard his advice, they jumped on the camels and raced to the city as fast as they could go. What advice did the wise man give them?

3. **The Farmer**

A farmer purchased a horse for $60. He sold it to his neighbor for $70. Then he found out that he could have made more money in a better deal. He went to his wife to borrow $10, and then bought the horse back for $80. The farmer then proceeded to sell the horse to another neighbor for $90. How much money did he make once all of the deals were complete?

4. **The Hour's Up**

If you have two hourglasses, one that measures 4 minutes and the other that measures 7 minutes, how could you use them to measure 9 minutes?

5. **The Hotel**

Three people checked into a room at a hotel. They paid the hotel manager $30 and went to their room. The manager figured out that the cost of the room should only have been $25 and gave the bellhop $5 to return to the group. On his way to the room, the bellboy decided that it would be hard to split $5 equally between three people, so he kept $2 for himself and gave $1 to each person.

Each of the 3 people had originally paid $10 for their share of the cost of the room. Now each person received $1 back in change, which meant that they paid $9 each, which totaled $27. The bellboy had $2, which meant that altogether $29 was accounted for. What happened to the remaining dollar?

Answers

You're probably curious as to how your logic skills measure up. Here's your chance to check your answers.

1. Ship-Wrecked

When the trains meet, they're both at the same spot, so both trains are exactly the same distance from New York City.

2. The Camels

The wise old man advised the brothers to switch camels with each other.

3. The Farmer

The farmer ended up with $90 from his final sale. He originally spent $60 on the horse when he bought it and he needed to return the $10 he borrowed to his wife. Those expenses add up to $70 which means he made $20 in profit ($90 - $70 = $20).

4. **The Hour's Up**

Start both hourglasses. When the 4 minute glass runs out, turn it over (4 minutes passed). When the 7 minute glass runs out, turn it over (7 minutes passed). When the 4 minute glass runs out the second time (8 minutes passed), this means that the 7 minute glass has been running for 1 minute. If you turn it over once again, it will measure one additional minute. When it stops, 9 minutes will have passed.

5. **The Hotel**

Each person paid $9, which totaled $27. The manager had $25 and the bellboy had $2 which means that all of the money is accounted for. If you add in the $1 given back to each person in change, the grand total is the $30 that was originally paid to the manager for the room. The bellboy's $2 should have been added to the manager's $25 or subtracted from the tenants' $27, not added to the tenants' $27.

Key Points:

- Logic is a way of reasonably looking at things and trying to understand them. Critical thinkers thrive on logic. Informal and formal logic are different ways of explaining an argument, and they are both useful in different situations.

- Informal logic is what critical thinkers use most often. It uses everyday language to make and evaluate real-life arguments. There is very little difference in the ways that males and females think and use this type of logic. Any negligible gaps in logic between the genders can be quickly and easily closed through education.

- We need to be on guard for the hidden assumptions held by others and ourselves as they impact the lens through which everyone views an argument. If we can recognize them, we can be more proactive in strengthening our arguments to be sure they aren't biased or invalid and be better prepared by conducting additional research to address the questions and concerns others may have as they challenge our conclusions.

Chapter 9: Reasoning by Analogy

Introducing reasoning by analogy

A cat is to mouse as a _____ is to a worm. If you ever had to answer questions like that, you just might have attended school in the United States. Chances are you have answered your fair share of analogy questions on tests throughout your academic career. But in the minds of some researchers who study the way our brains work, the ability to see the connection in analogies is key to strengthening our creativity and just might be responsible for some of the most amazing discoveries and inventions ever made. The ability to understand the connections illustrated in analogies is an important skill not only in school, but also in life. What are analogies and what makes them so important?

Analogies compare things that at first glance seem to be quite different from each other, but upon further examination have a connection between them or share some common traits. By highlighting a connection between things, analogies simplify and increase our understanding of more complex subjects by using a more familiar one to explain it.

Critical thinking tests were often made up of a lot of analogy questions like the one I gave earlier. Not all analogy questions are created equal, though. In the analogy: banana is to fruit as broccoli is to _____, it asks people to come up with the answer vegetable. This type of analogy is most concerned with measuring the ability of people to categorize objects and it would likely be found on simple logic tests.

In the analogy: cat is to mouse as _____ is to worm, it is a more open ended analogy and taps more into the creativity of the person answering it since it activates the imagination as it requires the consideration of a wider range of possibilities. In our example, one has to recognize the relationship between the cat and the mouse as the cat being a predator and the mouse being its prey and then consider from a large range of possibilities of what animal might have a predatory relationship with the worm as its prey. A bird, lizard, salamander, toad, ground beetle, turtle, frog, centipede, Eastern worm snake, pig, raccoon, otter, and weasel are a small sampling of the many animals that might fit into this analogy.

The second type of analogy would be more likely to appear on critical thinking tests because they understand how important the ability to decide which ideas are the most relevant from a vast selection of possibilities. The focus is on a deeper analysis.

The power of words

Words have power. The ability to express ourselves with language is one of the things that set us apart from other living things. Words allow us to communicate with one another and share ideas. They also play a role in the way we view the world as they are the foundation of the models we create in our minds.

Critical thinkers understand that words are not always easily understood because there are often many possible meanings for the same word. When choosing our own words or trying to understand the words others have chosen to use, a little careful analysis may be required.

While analogies are celebrated for their importance by many in the field of critical thinking, there are some, including renowned English philosophers John Locke and Thomas Hobbes. who were concerned at the ambiguity and imprecise language that sometimes come along with comparisons like analogies and metaphors. They believe it may get in the way of clear rational thought so revered in critical thinking. They acknowledge that analogies have their place and can play an important role in communication and debate as long as there is an attempt to be as precise as possible in our choice of words. When we aren't, we often require others to make big leaps in thinking. Critical thinkers don't appreciate that and our intended message may get lost in translation. Immanuel Kant, another great thinker, was quite fond of reasoning by analogies as he considered them the fruits of creative thinking.

Words are tricky. Often we may think that we are communicating with others in a perfectly clear, simple, and straightforward manner only to be surprised to find out that the message we were attempting to convey was very different from the message that was received by the listener.

Words are not always black and white. For example, consider the word happiness. It seems like a simple enough word that should easily be understood by everyone. It has played a big role in the United States throughout history and still today. Thomas Jefferson and the founding fathers felt so strongly about it that they included it in the Declaration of Independence as "life, liberty, and the pursuit of happiness" being unalienable rights.

To some, this may seem as though people were given permission to do anything they would like as long as it made them happy. There's definitely a political argument that one should be able to do pretty much anything as long as their rights don't infringe on another person. If I decide to populate my garden with ugly garden gnomes, and it doesn't infringe on other people, my gnomes should be legal. It's called Libertarianism. Destroying property, harming others, and stealing are just a few examples of unacceptable activities that the founding fathers did not intend to grant freedom to.

Even a word as seemingly simple and harmless as happiness can be open to a variety of interpretations, which can lead to unintended problems due its vagueness. As critical thinkers it is essential that we not only consider the literal definition of a word, but we also carefully examine the context in which it is used in order to determine the meaning behind it.

Uncovering false analogies

False analogies are everywhere. We may not even be aware of how many we are faced with in our daily lives. One area that intentionally uses false analogies in order to evoke a specific "feeling" in people is advertising. Advertisers compare very different things and try to show people that there is a connection between them when often there is not. Whether it is a commercial showing images that portray people drinking a particular brand of alcohol as being popular surrounded by successful attractive friends all laughing, happy, and having the time of their lives, or a political advertisement showing images of crime ridden poor cities that can be "expected" if people vote for a certain candidate, advertisers are experts at using false analogies to try to persuade people to agree with them.

Advertisers try to persuade others to agree with their point of view without actually presenting any evidence to support it. This can even happen in scientific debates.

An enduring debate that has occurred seemingly forever is about whether God, using a specific divine plan, created the universe, or through chance and a series of random events, when coupled with natural selection and survival of the fittest, ultimately lead to the universe as it currently exists. I will not rehash the debate or attempt to weigh in with my personal point of view. I will merely point out that those who believe in creationism often cite the famous watchmaker analogy stating that if there is design (instead of random chaos) in the universe that is proof that there must be a designer. One of the points they frequently make to add credence to their viewpoint is that the universe is too complex to have been created by chance and without an overarching plan. While it presents an interesting opinion to ponder, the analogy is not actual indisputable evidence, and as such it should be analyzed further, questioned, and challenged, not just immediately accepted at face value.

If you are aware that false analogies exist, you will want to make a conscious effort to ensure they do not interfere with your objective analysis as a critical thinker and carefully examine analogies to discover the connection highlighted in the comparison being made. This will help you see if the argument being made has merit.

Analogy in practice

Physicist, Niels Bohr, presented the Copenhagen Interpretation in 1920. His theory attempted to explain why the same subatomic particle might behave in different ways. Bohr believed these particles don't exist in one state or another, but rather in all possible states at the same time. He thought it was only when the particle was observed by someone that it was forced to take one state. In essence, the theory is that these incredibly tiny subatomic particles both exist and don't exist at the same time.[lx]

In 1935, Nobel Prize winning theoretical physicist, Erwin Schrödinger, thought the idea that whether or not something existed was dependent upon someone observing it was ridiculous, so he created his famous thought experiment known as Schrödinger's Cat. A thought experiment is one that is not physically conducted, but rather occurs within the imagination using reasoning.

In Schrödinger's Cat, a cat is placed in a sealed box for one hour along with a hammer, bottle of poison gas, radioactive atoms, and a Geiger counter. During the span of an hour, there would be a 50/50 chance that one of the atoms would decay and emit a particle. If it did, the Geiger counter would detect it and trigger the hammer to fall and break open the bottle of poison gas, which would kill the cat. If the atom didn't decay, the chain reaction would not occur, and the cat would still be alive once the box was opened. In this theory the cat is assumed to be both dead and alive (to exist and not exist) at the same time because no one is able to observe it and know for sure.[lxi]

Another famous thought experiment is Galileo's Balls. It was created by the Italian philosopher, mathematician, and astronomer, Galileo Galilei. In this experiment, the question being studied was if heavier objects fall faster than lighter objects. Galileo didn't believe it was necessary to physically drop objects in order to test this. He thought people had all of the information they needed and could arrive at the correct answer through reasoning.

The mental experiment involved Galileo climbing the Tower of Pisa and dropping two metal balls: one large and heavy and one smaller and light. Galileo was following one of Aristotle's laws, which stated that heavy objects fall faster than light objects. In the experiment, Galileo wanted to consider what would happen if a piece of string was tied between the two balls as they were dropped. He thought the lighter ball would act as a kind of parachute, causing both balls to fall more slowly than the heavier ball would fall independently.

Conversely, Galileo believed that if the lighter ball was held above the heavier ball, as they were tied together and dropped, their combined weights would equal a greater weight than the heavier ball alone, which would make them fall even faster. Since these two ideas stand in direct opposition to one another, Galileo's ultimate conclusion is that objects will fall at the same speed, regardless of their weight.

Galileo's thought experiment's conclusion came to be confirmed by physicists and played a crucial role in establishing future scientific theories and principles.[lxii]

Practice your analogy skills

Assess the strength of these analogical arguments presented by the Middle Way Society:

1. Cars are responsible for killing and injuring people just like guns. If you believe guns should be restricted because they are deadly weapons, then you should favor restrictions being placed on cars too.

2. If you are driving and someone is killed as a result of your reckless driving, you should face the possibility of a life sentence just like a murderer would. In both cases, the outcome is the same – a person died.

3. Annually, less people die from using ecstasy than from riding horses. Since taking ecstasy is less

dangerous than riding a horse, ecstasy shouldn't be illegal if riding horses isn't.

4. Some cultures practice arranged marriage. They defend the practice as being necessary since young people don't have the experience needed to wisely choose a partner. Even though they do not support arranged marriages, many people in Western culture use dating agencies or websites to select a partner. It is hypocritical for people who participate in those services to criticize the practice of arranged marriage.[lxiii]

Key Points:

- Even when we think we are being very clear and concise in our communication with others, there is the potential for the listener to receive a different message than we intend. We must choose our words carefully and try to avoid as much ambiguity as possible.

- Analogies can be great tools for categorizing, selecting relevant information, and even strengthening our creativity, but they are also susceptible to ambiguity and misinterpretation.

- False analogies also exist, particularly in the realm of advertising and politics, but also in debates over science as well. Sometimes people use false analogies to evoke certain emotions to try to persuade people to agree with their viewpoint without presenting any actual evidence to support it. It is important for critical thinkers to be on guard against this.

Chapter 10: Critical Thinking Hall of Fame

As we all strive to strengthen our own critical thinking skills, let's try to take a cue from some of the best critical thinkers the world has known. They have plenty they can teach us even today.

Critical thinking lessons from the greatest thinkers of the world:

Sir Isaac Newton

- Considered to be one of the most influential scientists of all time.

- Discovered gravity "by thinking on it continually."

- Was determined to analyze and test everything rigorously before accepting it as fact.

Lesson Learned: Be persistent. Question and challenge the world around you. You'll come up with better, more creative solutions than you ever imagined possible.

Marie Curie
- One of the world's most famous scientists.
- Two-time Nobel Prize winning physicist and chemist.
- Discovered radioactivity and the elements polonium and radium.
- Discoveries are used for x-rays and cancer treatment.

Lesson Learned: Asking the right questions are what critical thinking is all about. Critical thinking is digging deeper for evidence and not just accepting things at face value. You don't need to be negative to be a critical thinker just someone who trusts evidence.

Edwin Hubble

- Famous American astronomer who had the Hubble Space Telescope named after him.

- Discovered that there are galaxies beyond our Milky Way.

- Gathered and analyzed more data than any other scientist and proved the galaxies were expanding

- Found the farther away a galaxy is from Earth, the faster it seems to move away.

Lesson Learned: Critical thinking requires evidence and plenty of it. The more you have, the quicker you will be able to get to the heart of what's really going on, and the stronger your conclusions will be.

Simone de Beauvoir

- French writer, existentialist philosopher, political activist, and social theorist.

- The most revolutionary feminist thinker of the 20th century.

- Her 1949 book *The Second Sex* was the first work to argue for gender equality that celebrated a woman's individuality and voice.

Lesson Learned: Don't be afraid to think differently than the majority. You have to be willing to challenge even long held beliefs that act as the basis of society itself if need be.

Albert Einstein

- German born physicist and Nobel Prize winner.

- One of the world's most famous scientists best known for his Theory of Relativity.

- His scientific work was instrumental in the development of the atomic bomb, even though he wasn't personally involved.

Lesson Learned: Gather the facts, analyze them, and then trust your own judgment. If something looks wrong, it probably is. Dig deeper and find out why. Base your decisions and conclusions on the facts, not the assumptions of others. Chances are, you'll find a solution within the details.

Dr. Martin Luther King, Jr.
- Baptist minister, social activist, Nobel Prize winner, and famous orator.
- Fought for social justice through nonviolent means.
- Leader in the Civil Rights Movement from the 1950s until he was assassinated in 1968.
- Most famous for his "I have a dream" speech, which was a rallying cry for racial equality

that is still discussed and celebrated over fifty years after it was delivered.

Lesson Learned: If you want to make meaningful lasting change in the world, developing a strategy, crafting a well-thought out argument, and strengthen your persuasive skills.

Arguments that changed our world

Some arguments are so embedded in our culture and society that we rarely stop to think of where they came from in the first place or whether they are still valid and important today. As critical thinkers are keenly aware, all beliefs should be frequently reevaluated for their relevance and value. Let's take a look at a few of the arguments that have shaped our world.

The law should always be obeyed

This debate took center stage in the 17th century when English thinker and author, Thomas Hobbes, wrote in his book, *The Leviathan,* that governments should be able to treat their citizens any way they wished, because the only choice other than government control was anarchy and that would be much worse for people.

Hobbes argued that people are consumed with achieving power, fame, and fortune. He felt this inevitably would lead to competition and conflict, which could prove dangerous. His famous characterization of people as wolves roots in this idea. "Homo homini lupus est," in Latin means "A man is a wolf to another man." Hobbes thought the solution was for citizens to surrender their power to their government to prevent that from happening.

While Hobbes supported complete government control, today the argument has shifted to be about balancing citizens' rights with governmental authority. Hobbes thought that if people had too many rights the government would not have the power required to run things and chaos would ensue.

The problem with Hobbes's argument is that it was concerned with absolutes. He viewed government control as an all or nothing prospect: either the government would have total control or there would be complete anarchy. As we know from American democracy, it is certainly possible to find a happy medium. The government can have the rule of law to keep things orderly and safe while at the same time recognizing the individual's rights.[lxiv]

Actions of a greedy elite contribute to the suffering of average people

This argument was championed in the mid 19th century by Karl Marx and Friedrich Engels in their book, the *Communist Manifesto*. At that time in history, there was a vastly different reality between the experiences of the elite, wealthy farmers and factory workers and the very poor working class.

They argued that distinguishing between economic classes needed to be abandoned in order to make everyone equal. They thought the general population needed power in order to eliminate the ruling elite.

Even in their effort to eliminate the control of the ruling upper class, they ended up creating another elite class that was supposed to monitor the situation and act in the best interest of the common people. That group of elites was also ultimately influenced by greed and didn't always look out for the average people.

The problem is even when an attempt to eliminate class was made, a divide between those in positions of authority and the common people in society still existed.[lxv]

For the good of all, only a select few are qualified to hold positions of power

Plato made this argument over 2,000 years ago in *The Republic*. He referred to those who should be in power as the Guardians and he believed that it was a small group of intelligent people who had the desire to serve others. Plato felt that most people didn't have the knowledge necessary to help run a society.

He suggested that the majority of people would be content and willing to go along with this notion as long as they were regularly told how well things were going and how the actions of those in power were benefitting them. Remember, propaganda comes from only providing people with one source of information and expecting them to accept what they are being told without question.

The problem with this argument is that even though the ruling elites might start out with the best of intentions to serve the public, greed will always enter in some fashion and impact the decisions made. Eventually, the masses will become disenchanted and attempt to respond. Democracy and the rule of law created a safe way for people to express their frustration and have conflicts with one another. Even today, there are countries with ruling elites that keep their populations in check by controlling the information they receive by mandating what can be taught in schools and what can be shared in the media.[lxvi]

Einstein's theory of relativity

While the theory of relativity was a thought experiment, it is also an argument that has impacted the way people view the world. Albert Einstein made this argument over 100 years ago. It addressed what happens with time when travel occurs at or very close to the speed of light. Einstein believed that the laws of physics dictated that clocks traveling close to the speed of light would actually move slower than clocks that were stationary.

If you extended Einstein's assumption to human travel in space, one could travel to the closest star and back, moving near the speed of light, and age ten years. During that same span of time, everyone else who had remained on Earth would have aged twenty years.

The problem with this argument is that, in continuing with our space travel example, if the person traveling in space looked back at Earth from their spaceship, those on Earth would be in motion in relation to the one in space. As a result, the people on Earth should be the ones aging more slowly. Einstein, along with other scientists, tried to address this question, but have been unable to completely do so.[lxvii]

There are many lessons that we, as critical thinkers, can learn from those who have come before us and the arguments that have had such a major impact on the way in which we view the world. It is us to us as to whether we will take advantage of the wealth of knowledge at our fingertips.

Closing

We live in a time where we have access to more data and information at our fingertips than ever before. This can be overwhelming when our brains are hardwired to look for quick and easy solutions to conserve as much energy as possible. This brain energy-saver mode makes us susceptible to falling into old habits and staying in our comfort zone of holding on to beliefs and ideas that have long since outlived their relevance and helpfulness. It puts us at risk of only looking at ideas and information that affirm our preexisting viewpoints and dismissing those that dispute it. It opens us up to the possibility of falling for propaganda and being indoctrinated into negative or dangerous lines of thinking.

Critical thinkers recognize that we are constantly inundated with messages trying to persuade us to think, vote, and act in certain ways. They look for biases, gaps in information, and errors in reasoning in both themselves and others that can cloud their judgment. They are aware of the language and persuasive techniques that people utilize in an attempt to influence each other daily. Strong critical thinkers understand that so many of our thoughts are guided by emotions, which open us up to being easily influenced by others instead of deliberate rational thought. They fight against this because they know how important it is to be able to make the best and most informed decisions possible.

There are so many benefits that come from being a critical thinker. From being able to take ownership of our own thoughts and learning, to making objective informed decisions, to being receptive and sympathetic to viewpoints that differ from our own, and everything else in between. Strengthening our critical thinking skills can enhance our lives for the better in countless ways if we choose to let it.

Being a critical thinker isn't something that necessarily comes naturally to us. But if we are willing to make the conscious choice every day to dig deeper and search for evidence; be receptive to the possibility of gaining knowledge from a variety of sources and viewpoints, not just the ones that affirm the views we already have; to be willing to challenge opinions disguised as facts from everyone, including those in authority deemed as experts; and those we admire and respect by asking the right questions, we can reap great rewards. It requires extra time, effort, and energy on our part, but we get out of life what we put into it. If we are willing to put in the work, the world will make sense a little bit more.

Thank you for reading this book and allowing me to share in a portion of your critical thinking journey. I wish you all the best as you continue on your path of lifelong learning and seek to find real knowledge and truth.

Reference

Alpha History. Hitler On Propaganda (1924). Alpha History. 2018.
https://alphahistory.com/nazigermany/hitler-on-propaganda-1924/

Andrew S. Wigosky. RAPID Value Management for the Business Cost of Ownership. Digital Press. p. 5. ISBN 9781555582890. 2004.

Atkin, Albert. Peirce's Theory of Signs. Stanford Encyclopedia of Philosophy. 2016.
https://plato.stanford.edu/entries/peirce-semiotics/

Baird, Forrest E.; Walter Kaufmann. From Plato to Derrida. Upper Saddle River, New Jersey: Pearson Prentice Hall. ISBN 978-0-13-158591-1. 2008.

Bellinger, Gene. Castro, Durvall. Mills, Anthony. Data, Information, Knowledge, and Wisdom. Systems Thinking. 2004. http://www.systems-thinking.org/dikw/dikw.htm

Biswas-Diener, Robert. Kashdan Todd B. What Happy People Do Differently? Psychology Today. 2013. https://www.psychologytoday.com/us/articles/201307/what-happy-people-do-differently

Brogaard, Berit. PhD. Linda The Bank Teller Case Revisited. Psychology Today. 2016. https://www.psychologytoday.com/us/blog/the-superhuman-mind/201611/linda-the-bank-teller-case-revisited

Browne, Alex. Social Darwinism in Nazi Germany. History Hit. 2018. https://www.historyhit.com/social-darwinism-in-nazi-germany/

Castronovo, Russ. Propaganda 1776: Secrets, Leaks, and Revolutionary Communications in Early America (Oxford Studies in American Literary History). Oxford University Press. 2014.

Centre For Public Impact. Tackling the Declining Birth Rate in Japan. Centre For Public Impact. 2017. https://www.centreforpublicimpact.org/case-study/tackling-declining-birth-rate-japan/

Cohn, Norman. Warrant for Genocide, The myth of the Jewish world conspiracy and the 'Protocols of the Elders of Zion', Eyre & Spottiswoode, ISBN 1-897959-25-7. 1967.

Cole, Niki Lisa PhD. Definition of Idiographic and Nomothetic. Thought Co. 2018. https://www.thoughtco.com/nomothetic-3026355

Correia, Vasco. Biases and fallacies: The role of motivated irrationality in fallacious reasoning. Vasco Correia. 2018.
https://pdfs.semanticscholar.org/7f27/529ac93c3d86bd2b251d1787c63f0d10fb3c.pdf

Critical – Define Critical at Dictionary.com. Dictionary.com. Retrieved in 20.08.2018.

Dewey, John. Individual Psychology And Education. The Philosopher, Volume. XII, 1934. The Philosopher. 2000.
http://www.the-philosopher.co.uk/2016/08/individual-psychology-and-education-1934.html

Derbyshire, David. Colgate gets the brush off for 'misleading' ads. The Telegraph. 2007.
https://www.telegraph.co.uk/news/uknews/1539715/Colgate-gets-the-brush-off-for-misleading-ads.html

Dewey, John. John Dewey, The Later Works, 1925-1953. Volume 9; 1933-1934. Southern Illinois University Press. 1986.

DeWitt, Peter. What's Our Best Taxonomy? Bloom's or SOLO? Education Week. 2014. http://blogs.edweek.org/edweek/finding_common_ground/2014/02/whats_our_best_taxonomy_blooms_or_solo.html

Drake, Stillman. Galileo at Work: His Scientific Biography (Facsim. ed.). Mineola (N.Y.): Dover publ. ISBN 9780486495422. 2003.

Dunning, D., Meyerowitz, J., & Holzberg, A. Ambiguity and Self-Evaluation: The Role of Idiosyncratic Trait Definitions in Self-Serving Assessments of Ability. In T. Gilovich, D. Griffin, & D. Kahneman (Eds.), Heuristics and Biases: The Psychology of Intuitive Judgment (pp. 324-333). Cambridge: Cambridge University Press.

doi:10.1017/CBO9780511808098.020. 2002. https://www.cambridge.org/core/books/heuristics-and-biases/ambiguity-and-selfevaluation-the-role-of-idiosyncratic-trait-definitions-in-selfserving-assessments-of-ability/AD02843FDFE75A167603DA6469565562

Einstein, Albert. On the Electrodynamics of Moving Bodies. Annalen der Physik. 17 (10): 891. Bibcode: 1905AnP.322.891E. doi:10.1002/andp.19053221004. 1905.

Elder, Linda. Paul, Richard. The Analysis & Assessment of Thinking. Critical Thinking. 2017. http://www.criticalthinking.org/pages/the-analysis-amp-assessment-of-thinking/497

Ellis, Robert M. Critical Thinking 12: Analogies. Middle Way Society. 2014. http://www.middlewaysociety.org/critical-thinking-12-analogies/

Faye, Jan. Copenhagen Interpretation of Quantum Mechanics. Stanford Encyclopedia of Philosophy. 2014. https://plato.stanford.edu/entries/qm-copenhagen/

Flannery, Maura C. Observations on biology (PDF). The American Biology Teacher. 69 (9): 561–564. doi:10.1662/0002-7685(2007)69[561:OOB]2.0.CO. 2007.

Forehand, M. Bloom's taxonomy: Original and revised. In M. Orey (Ed.), Emerging perspectives on learning, teaching, and technology. 2005. http://projects.coe.uga.edu/epltt/

Goldfarb, Zachary A. These four charts show how the SAT favors rich, educated families. The Washington Post. 2014. https://www.washingtonpost.com/news/wonk/wp/2014/03/05/these-four-charts-show-how-the-sat-favors-the-rich-educated-families/?utm_term=.a6cd8a96e40b

Graves, Christopher. Part One: We Are Not Thinking Machines. We Are Feeling Machines That Think. Institute for Public Relations. 2015. https://instituteforpr.org/part-one-not-thinking-machines-feeling-machines-think/

Hartland S. Snyder. Cascade Theory. Phys. Rev. 75, 906. 1949. https://journals.aps.org/pr/abstract/10.1103/PhysRev.75.906.2

Hawking, Stephen. On the Shoulders of Giants. Running Press. p. 731. ISBN 0-7624-1698-X. 2003.

Hinton, David B. Triumph of the Will: Document or Artifice? Cinema Journal. University of Texas Press. 15 (1): 48–57. doi:10.2307/1225104. JSTOR 1225104. 1975.

Hitler, Adolf. Mein Kampf. Chapter 10. Adolf Hitler. 2018. http://www.hitler.org/writings/Mein_Kampf/mkv1ch10.html

HookEd. Advantages of SOLO Taxonomy. HookEd. 2017. http://pamhook.com/wiki/Advantages_of_SOLO_Taxonomy

Hugh G. Gauch, Scientific Method in Practice, Cambridge University Press. ISBN 0-521-01708-4, ISBN 978-0-521-01708-4. 2003.

IFL Science. Schrödinger's Cat: Explained. IFL Science. 2018. https://www.iflscience.com/physics/schrödinger's-cat-explained/

Insight Assessment. Characteristics of Strong Critical Thinkers. Insight Assessment. 2018. https://www.insightassessment.com/Resources/Importance-of-Critical-Thinking/Characteristics-of-Strong-Critical-Thinkers

Kahneman, Daniel. Thinking, Fast and Slow. Penguin. 2011.

Kuhn, Deanna. Shaughnessy, Michael E. Educational Psychology Review. Vol. 16, No. 3, pp. 267-282. 2004. https://www.jstor.org/stable/23363860

Mages Blog. Hit and run. Think Bayes! Mages Blog. 2014. https://magesblog.com/post/2014-07-29-hit-and-run-think-bayes/

Mark U. Edwards, Printing Propaganda and Martin Luther 15; Louise W. Holborn, "Printing and the Growth of a Protestant Movement in Germany from 1517 to 1524", Church History, 11, no. 2. 1942.

McDonald, David. The Racist Roots of Marijuana Prohibition. Foundation for Economic Education. 2017. https://fee.org/articles/the-racist-roots-of-marijuana-prohibition/

Med Shadow. Drug Classification. Med Shadow. 2017. https://medshadow.org/resource/drug-classifications-schedule-ii-iii-iv-v/

Mehring, Franz, Karl Marx: The Story of His Life. Routledge. 2003.

MSU. Transition Words. MSU. 2018. https://msu.edu/~jdowell/135/transw.html

Nagle, D. Brendan; Stanley M Burstein. The Ancient World: Readings in Social and Cultural History. Pearson Education. p. 133. ISBN 978-0-205-69187-6. 2009.

New Mexico Media Literacy Project. The Language of Persuasion. New Mexico Media Literacy Project. 2007.
https://www.greenwichschools.org/uploaded/faculty/maryellen_brezovsky/CMS/8_Media_Literacy/The_Language_of_Persuasion.pdf

Paul, R. Critical thinking: what every person needs to survive in a rapidly changing world (3rd ed.). Rohnert Park, California: Sonoma State University Press. 1993.

Philosi Blog. A great many people think they are thinking when they are merely rearranging their prejudices. Philosi Blog. 2012.
https://philosiblog.com/2012/05/10/a-great-many-people-think-they-are-thinking-when-they-are-merely-rearranging-their-prejudices/

PsycholoGenie Staff. Thought Process in Humans: Concrete Vs. Abstract Thinking. PsycholoGenie.

2018. https://psychologenie.com/concrete-vs-abstract-thinking

Raichle, Marcus E. Gusnard, Debra A. Appraising the brain's energy budget. Proceedings of the National Academy of Sciences, 99 (16) 10237-10239; DOI: 10.1073/pnas.172399499. 2002. http://www.pnas.org/content/99/16/10237

Research Gate. What advantages has Solo taxonomy over Bloom's taxonomy or vice versa? Research Gate. 2016. https://www.researchgate.net/post/What_advantages_has_Solo_taxonomy_over_Blooms_taxonomy_or_vice_versa

Shea, Brendan. Karl Popper: Philosophy of Science. Internet Encyclopedia of Philosophy. 2018. https://www.iep.utm.edu/pop-sci/

Sheldon, Dr. Garrett Ward. The History of Political Theory: Ancient Greece to Modern America. Peter Lang. p. 253. ISBN 9780820423005. 2003.

Soll, Jack B. Milkman, Katherine L., Payne, John W. A User's Guide To Debiasing.
2018.
http://www.opim.wharton.upenn.edu/~kmilkman/Soll_et_al_2013.pdf

St. B. T. Evans, Jonathan & L. Barston, Julie & Pollard, Paul. On the Conflict between Logic and Belief in Syllogistic Reasoning. Memory & cognition. 11. 295-306. 10.3758/BF03196976. 1983. https://www.researchgate.net/publication/16575665_On_the_Conflict_between_Logic_and_Belief_in_Syllogistic_Reasoning

Sullivan, Jenie. How Does Bloom's Taxonomy Relate to Critical Thinking Information? Classroom. 2018.

https://classroom.synonym.com/blooms-relate-critical-thinking-information-6233382.html

Teachnology. Logic Puzzle Worksheets. Teachnology. 2018. http://www.teach-nology.com/worksheets/critical_thinking/logic/

Teaching and Educational Development Institute. Biggs' structure of the observed learning outcome (SOLO) taxonomy. University of Queensland. 2018. http://www.uq.edu.au/teach/assessment/docs/biggs-SOLO.pdf

Thinking Writing. Non-Critical And Critical Approaches. Thinking Writing. 2018. http://www.thinkingwriting.qmul.ac.uk/non-critical/critical

University of Louisville. Paul-Elder Critical Thinking Framework. University of Louisville. 2018.

http://louisville.edu/ideastoaction/about/criticalthinking/framework

WW Norton. Hypothetical Syllogisms: Affirming the Antecedent (Modus ponens). WW Norton & Co. 1998.
https://www.wwnorton.com/college/phil/logic3/ch10/affante.htm

WW Norton. Hypothetical Syllogisms: Denying the Consequent. (Modus Tollens). WW Norton & Co. 1998.
https://www.wwnorton.com/college/phil/logic3/ch10/denycons.htm

Endnotes

[i] "Critical – Define Critical at Dictionary.com". Dictionary.com. Retrieved in 20.08.2018.
[ii] Insight Assessment. Characteristics of Strong Critical Thinkers. Insight Assessment. 2018. https://www.insightassessment.com/Resources/Importance-of-Critical-Thinking/Characteristics-of-Strong-Critical-Thinkers
[iii] Atkin, Albert. Peirce's Theory of Signs. Stanford Encyclopedia of Philosophy. 2016. https://plato.stanford.edu/entries/peirce-semiotics/
[iv] Philosi Blog. A great many people think they are thinking when they are merely rearranging their prejudices. Philosi Blog. 2012. https://philosiblog.com/2012/05/10/a-great-many-people-think-they-are-thinking-when-they-are-merely-rearranging-their-prejudices/
[v] Kahneman, Daniel. Thinking, Fast and Slow. Penguin. 2011.
[vi] Raichle, Marcus E. Gusnard, Debra A. Appraising the brain's energy budget. Proceedings of the National Academy of Sciences, 99 (16) 10237-10239; DOI: 10.1073/pnas.172399499. 2002. http://www.pnas.org/content/99/16/10237

[vii] Kuhn, Deanna. Shaughnessy, Michael E. Educational Psychology Review. Vol. 16, No. 3, pp. 267-282. 2004. https://www.jstor.org/stable/23363860

[viii] Hartland S. Snyder. Cascade Theory. Phys. Rev. 75, 906. 1949. https://journals.aps.org/pr/abstract/10.1103/PhysRev.75.906.2

[ix] Derbyshire, David. Colgate gets the brush off for 'misleading' ads. The Telegraph. 2007. https://www.telegraph.co.uk/news/uknews/1539715/Colgate-gets-the-brush-off-for-misleading-ads.html

[x] Thinking Writing. Non-Critical And Critical Approaches. Thinking Writing. 2018. http://www.thinkingwriting.qmul.ac.uk/non-critical/critical

[xi] Brogaard, Berit. PhD. Linda The Bank Teller Case Revisited. Psychology Today. 2016. https://www.psychologytoday.com/us/blog/the-superhuman-mind/201611/linda-the-bank-teller-case-revisited

[xii] Kahneman, Daniel. Thinking, Fast and Slow. Penguin. 2011.

[xiii] Mages Blog. Hit and run. Think Bayes! Mages Blog. 2014. https://magesblog.com/post/2014-07-29-hit-and-run-think-bayes/

[xiv] Goldfarb, Zachary A. These four charts show how the SAT favors rich, educated families. The Washington Post. 2014. https://www.washingtonpost.com/news/wonk/wp/2014/03/05/these-four-charts-show-how-the-sat-favors-

the-rich-educated-families/?utm_term=.a6cd8a96e40b
[xv] Correia, Vasco. Biases and fallacies: The role of motivated irrationality in fallacious reasoning. Vasco Correia. 2018. https://pdfs.semanticscholar.org/7f27/529ac93c3d86bd2b251d1787c63f0d10fb3c.pdf
[xvi] Biswas-Diener, Robert. Kashdan Todd B. What Happy People Do Differently? Psychology Today. 2013. https://www.psychologytoday.com/us/articles/201307/what-happy-people-do-differently
[xvii] Dunning, D., Meyerowitz, J., & Holzberg, A. Ambiguity and Self-Evaluation: The Role of Idiosyncratic Trait Definitions in Self-Serving Assessments of Ability. In T. Gilovich, D. Griffin, & D. Kahneman (Eds.), Heuristics and Biases: The Psychology of Intuitive Judgment (pp. 324-333). Cambridge: Cambridge University Press. doi:10.1017/CBO9780511808098.020. 2002. https://www.cambridge.org/core/books/heuristics-and-biases/ambiguity-and-selfevaluation-the-role-of-idiosyncratic-trait-definitions-in-selfserving-assessments-of-ability/AD02843FDFE75A167603DA6469565562
[xviii] St. B. T. Evans, Jonathan & L. Barston, Julie & Pollard, Paul. On the Conflict between Logic and Belief in Syllogistic Reasoning. Memory & cognition. 11. 295-306. 10.3758/BF03196976. 1983. https://www.researchgate.net/publication/16575665_

On_the_Conflict_between_Logic_and_Belief_in_Syllogistic_Reasoning

[xix] Shea, Brendan. Karl Popper: Philosophy of Science. Internet Encyclopedia of Philosophy. 2018. https://www.iep.utm.edu/pop-sci/

[xx] Nagle, D. Brendan; Stanley M Burstein. The Ancient World: Readings in Social and Cultural History. Pearson Education. p. 133. ISBN 978-0-205-69187-6. 2009.

[xxi] Mark U. Edwards, Printing Propaganda and Martin Luther 15; Louise W. Holborn, "Printing and the Growth of a Protestant Movement in Germany from 1517 to 1524", Church History, 11, no. 2. 1942.

[xxii] Castronovo, Russ. Propaganda 1776: Secrets, Leaks, and Revolutionary Communications in Early America (Oxford Studies in American Literary History). Oxford University Press. 2014.

[xxiii] Cohn, Norman. Warrant for Genocide, The myth of the Jewish world conspiracy and the 'Protocols of the Elders of Zion', Eyre & Spottiswoode, ISBN 1-897959-25-7. 1967.

[xxiv] Hinton, David B. Triumph of the Will: Document or Artifice? Cinema Journal. University of Texas Press. 15 (1): 48–57. doi:10.2307/1225104. JSTOR 1225104. 1975.

[xxv] Alpha History. Hitler On Propaganda (1924). Alpha History. 2018. https://alphahistory.com/nazigermany/hitler-on-propaganda-1924/

[xxvi] Graves, Christopher. Part One: We Are Not Thinking Machines. We Are Feeling Machines That Think. Institute for Public Relations. 2015. https://instituteforpr.org/part-one-not-thinking-machines-feeling-machines-think/
[xxvii] Hitler, Adolf. Mein Kampf. Chapter 10. Adolf Hitler. 2018. http://www.hitler.org/writings/Mein_Kampf/mkv1ch10.html
[xxviii] Browne, Alex. Social Darwinism in Nazi Germany. History Hit. 2018. https://www.historyhit.com/social-darwinism-in-nazi-germany/
[xxix] McDonald, David. The Racist Roots of Marijuana Prohibition. Foundation for Economic Education. 2017. https://fee.org/articles/the-racist-roots-of-marijuana-prohibition/
[xxx] Med Shadow. Drug Classification. Med Shadow. 2017. https://medshadow.org/resource/drug-classifications-schedule-ii-iii-iv-v/
[xxxi] New Mexico Media Literacy Project. The Language of Persuasion. New Mexico Media Literacy Project. 2007. https://www.greenwichschools.org/uploaded/faculty/maryellen_brezovsky/CMS/8_Media_Literacy/The_Language_of_Persuasion.pdf
[xxxii] New Mexico Media Literacy Project. The Language of Persuasion. New Mexico Media Literacy Project. 2007. https://www.greenwichschools.org/uploaded/faculty/

maryellen_brezovsky/CMS/8_Media_Literacy/The_Language_of_Persuasion.pdf

[xxxiii] Sullivan, Jenie. How Does Bloom's Taxonomy Relate to Critical Thinking Information? Classroom. 2018. https://classroom.synonym.com/blooms-relate-critical-thinking-information-6233382.html

[xxxiv] Forehand, M. Bloom's taxonomy: Original and revised. In M. Orey (Ed.), Emerging perspectives on learning, teaching, and technology. 2005. http://projects.coe.uga.edu/epltt/

[xxxv] Paul, R. Critical thinking: what every person needs to survive in a rapidly changing world (3rd ed.). Rohnert Park, California: Sonoma State University Press. 1993.

[xxxvi] Flannery, Maura C. Observations on biology (PDF). The American Biology Teacher. 69 (9): 561–564. doi:10.1662/0002-7685(2007)69[561:OOB]2.0.CO. 2007.

[xxxvii] Teaching and Educational Development Institute. Biggs' structure of the observed learning outcome (SOLO) taxonomy. University of Queensland. 2018. http://www.uq.edu.au/teach/assessment/docs/biggs-SOLO.pdf

[xxxviii] DeWitt, Peter. What's Our Best Taxonomy? Bloom's or SOLO? Education Week. 2014. http://blogs.edweek.org/edweek/finding_common_ground/2014/02/whats_our_best_taxonomy_blooms_or_solo.html

[xxxix] Research Gate. What advantages has Solo taxonomy over Bloom's taxonomy or vice versa?

Research Gate. 2016. https://www.researchgate.net/post/What_advantages_has_Solo_taxonomy_over_Blooms_taxonomy_or_vice_versa

[xl] HookEd. Advantages of SOLO Taxonomy. HookEd. 2017. http://pamhook.com/wiki/Advantages_of_SOLO_Taxonomy

[xli] University of Louisville. Paul-Elder Critical Thinking Framework. University of Louisville. 2018. http://louisville.edu/ideastoaction/about/criticalthinking/framework

[xlii] Elder, Linda. Paul, Richard. The Analysis & Assessment of Thinking. Critical Thinking. 2017. http://www.criticalthinking.org/pages/the-analysis-amp-assessment-of-thinking/497

[xliii] University of Louisville. Paul-Elder Critical Thinking Framework. University of Louisville. 2018. http://louisville.edu/ideastoaction/about/criticalthinking/framework

[xliv] Hugh G. Gauch, Scientific Method in Practice, Cambridge University Press. ISBN 0-521-01708-4, ISBN 978-0-521-01708-4. 2003.

[xlv] Hawking, Stephen. On the Shoulders of Giants. Running Press. p. 731. ISBN 0-7624-1698-X. 2003.

[xlvi] Andrew S. Wigosky. RAPID Value Management for the Business Cost of Ownership. Digital Press. p. 5. ISBN 9781555582890. 2004.

[xlvii] Kahneman, Daniel. Thinking, Fast and Slow. Penguin. 2011.

[xlviii] PsycholoGenie Staff. Thought Process in Humans: Concrete Vs. Abstract Thinking. PsycholoGenie. 2018. https://psychologenie.com/concrete-vs-abstract-thinking

[xlix] Bellinger, Gene. Castro, Durvall. Mills, Anthony. Data, Information, Knowledge, and Wisdom. Systems Thinking. 2004. http://www.systems-thinking.org/dikw/dikw.htm

[l] Dewey, John. Individual Psychology And Education. The Philosopher, Volume. XII, 1934. The Philosopher. 2000. http://www.the-philosopher.co.uk/2016/08/individual-psychology-and-education-1934.html

[li] Dewey, John. John Dewey, The Later Works, 1925-1953. Volume 9; 1933-1934. Southern Illinois University Press. 1986.

[lii] Dewey, John. John Dewey, The Later Works, 1925-1953. Volume 9; 1933-1934. Southern Illinois University Press. 1986.

[liii] Soll, Jack B. Milkman, Katherine L., Payne, John W. A User's Guide To Debiasing. 2018. http://www.opim.wharton.upenn.edu/~kmilkman/Soll_et_al_2013.pdf

[liv] Cole, Niki Lisa PhD. Definition of Idiographic and Nomothetic. Thought Co. 2018. https://www.thoughtco.com/nomothetic-3026355

[lv] MSU. Transition Words. MSU. 2018. https://msu.edu/~jdowell/135/transw.html

[lvi] Centre For Public Impact. Tackling the Declining Birth Rate in Japan. Centre For Public Impact. 2017.

https://www.centreforpublicimpact.org/case-study/tackling-declining-birth-rate-japan/
[lvii] WW Norton. Hypothetical Syllogisms: Affirming the Antecedent (Modus ponens). WW Norton & Co. 1998. https://www.wwnorton.com/college/phil/logic3/ch10/affante.htm
[lviii] WW Norton. Hypothetical Syllogisms: Denying the Consequent. (Modus Tollens). WW Norton & Co. 1998. https://www.wwnorton.com/college/phil/logic3/ch10/denycons.htm
[lix] Teachnology. Logic Puzzle Worksheets. Teachnology. 2018. http://www.teach-nology.com/worksheets/critical_thinking/logic/
[lx] Faye, Jan. Copenhagen Interpretation of Quantum Mechanics. Stanford Encyclopedia of Philosophy. 2014. https://plato.stanford.edu/entries/qm-copenhagen/
[lxi] IFL Science. Schrödinger's Cat: Explained. IFL Science. 2018. https://www.iflscience.com/physics/schrödinger's-cat-explained/
[lxii] Drake, Stillman. Galileo at Work: His Scientific Biography (Facsim. ed.). Mineola (N.Y.): Dover publ. ISBN 9780486495422. 2003.
[lxiii] Ellis, Robert M. Critical Thinking 12: Analogies. Middle Way Society. 2014. http://www.middlewaysociety.org/critical-thinking-12-analogies/

[lxiv] Sheldon, Dr. Garrett Ward. The History of Political Theory: Ancient Greece to Modern America. Peter Lang. p. 253. ISBN 9780820423005. 2003.
[lxv] Mehring, Franz, Karl Marx: The Story of His Life. Routledge. 2003.
[lxvi] Baird, Forrest E.; Walter Kaufmann. From Plato to Derrida. Upper Saddle River, New Jersey: Pearson Prentice Hall. ISBN 978-0-13-158591-1. 2008.
[lxvii] Einstein, Albert. On the Electrodynamics of Moving Bodies. Annalen der Physik. 17 (10): 891. Bibcode: 1905AnP.322.891E. doi:10.1002/andp.19053221004. 1905.

Made in the USA
Columbia, SC
13 February 2020